GREATEST EVER

Pasta

This is a Papplewick Press Book
First published in 2002

Papplewick Press
Unit 5 Bestwood Business Park
Bestwood Village
Nottingham NG6 8AN, UK

ISBN: 0-75259-093-6

Printed in Dubai

Produced by The Bridgewater Book Company Ltd

NOTE

This book uses metric and imperial measurements. Follow the same units
of measurement throughout; do not mix metric and imperial.
All spoon measurements are level: teaspoons are assumed to be 5 ml,
and tablespoons are assumed to be 15 ml. Unless otherwise stated,
milk is assumed to be full fat, eggs and individual vegetables such as potatoes
are medium, and pepper is freshly ground black pepper.

The times given for each recipe are an
approximate guide only because the preparation times may differ according
to the techniques used by different people and the cooking times may vary
as a result of the type of oven used.

Recipes using raw or very lightly cooked eggs should be
avoided by infants, the elderly, pregnant women, convalescents, and anyone
suffering from an illness.

Contents

Introduction

Pasta has existed in one form or another since the days

of the Roman Empire and it remains one of the most

versatile ingredients in the kitchen. It can be combined

with almost anything from meat to fish, vegetables to

fruit and is even delicious served with simple herb

sauces. No store cupboard should be without a supply of dried pasta, which,

combined with a few other stock ingredients, can be turned into a mouth-

watering and nutritious meal within minutes.

Most pasta is made from durum wheat flour and contains protein and

carbohydrates. It is a good source of slow-release energy and has the

additional advantage of being value for money.

There is an enormous range of different types of pasta. Many are available

both dried and fresh. Unless you have access to a good Italian delicatessen,

it is probably not worth buying fresh unfilled pasta, but even supermarkets sell

high-quality tortellini, capelletti, ravioli and agnolotti.

Best of all, make fresh pasta at home. It takes a little time, but is quite easy

and worth the effort. You can mix the dough by hand or in a food processor.

Pasta Shapes

There are thought to be at least 200 different shapes of pasta with over 600 different names. New varieties are being designed constantly and the same shape may have different names in different regions of Italy. Basically, pasta falls into four categories: long round, long ribbons, tubes and small shapes. Pasta may also be stuffed with a variety of fillings. The following is a list of some of the most frequently used types of unfilled pasta.

Cravatte, Cravattini bows
Cresti Di Gallo 'cock's comb', curved shapes
Dischi Volante 'flying saucers'
Ditali, Ditalini 'little thimbles', short tubes
Eliche loose, spiral shapes
Elicoidali short, ridge tubes
Farfalle bows
Fedeli, Fedelini fine tubes twisted into skeins
Festonati short lengths, like festoons
Fettuccine narrow ribbon pasta
Fiochette, Fiochelli small bows
Frezine broad, flat ribbons
Fusilli spindles or short spirals
Fusilli Bucati thin spirals, like springs
Gemelli, 'twins', two pieces wrapped together

Gramigna meaning 'grass' or 'weed', look like sprouting seeds from Emilia Romagna
Lasagne flat, rectangular sheets
Linguine long, flat ribbons
Lumache smooth, snail-like shells
Lumachine U-shaped flat pasta
Macaroni, Maccheroni long or short-cut tubes, may be ridged or elbow-shaped
Maltagliati triangular
Orecchiette ear-shaped
Orzi tiny, rice-like grains
Pappardelle widest ribbons, straight with sawtooth edges
Pearlini tiny discs
Penne quills, short, thick tubes with diagonally cut ends

Pipe Rigate ridged, curved pipe shapes
Rigatoni thick, ridged tubes
Rotelle wheels
Ruote wheels
Semini seed shapes
Spaghetti fine, medium and thick rods
Spirale two rods twisted into spirals
Strozzapreti 'priest strangler', double twisted strands
Tagliarini flat ribbons, thinner than tagliatelle
Tagliatelle broad, flat ribbons
Tortiglione thin, twisted tubes
Vermicelli fine, slender strands usually twisted into skeins
Ziti Tagliati short, thick tubes

Basic Recipes

Fresh Chicken Stock

MAKES 1.7 LITRES/3 PINTS

1 kg/2 lb 4 oz chicken, skinned

2 celery sticks

1 onion

2 carrots

1 garlic clove

few fresh parsley sprigs

2 litres/3½ pints water

salt and pepper

1 Put all the ingredients into a large pan and bring to the boil over a medium heat.

2 Using a slotted spoon, skim away any scum on the surface. Reduce the heat to a gentle simmer, partially cover and cook for 2 hours, then leave to cool.

3 Line a sieve with clean muslin and put over a large jug or bowl. Pour the stock through the sieve. The cooked chicken can be used in another recipe. Discard the other solids. Cover the stock and chill in the refrigerator.

4 Skim away any fat that forms before using. Store in the refrigerator for 3–4 days until required or freeze in small batches.

Fresh Vegetable Stock

This can be kept chilled for up to 3 days or frozen for up to 3 months. Salt is not added when cooking the stock: it is better to season it according to the dish in which it is to be used.

MAKES 1.5 LITRES/2¾ PINTS

250 g/9 oz shallots

1 large carrot, diced

1 celery stick, chopped

½ fennel bulb

1 garlic clove

1 bay leaf

a few fresh parsley and tarragon sprigs

2 litres/ 3½ pints water

pepper

1 Put all the ingredients into a large pan and bring to the boil over a medium heat.

2 Using a slotted spoon, skim off any scum on the surface. Reduce the heat to a gentle simmer, partially cover and cook for 45 minutes, then leave to cool.

3 Line a sieve with clean muslin and put over a large jug or bowl. Pour the stock through the sieve. Discard the herbs and vegetables.

4 Cover and store in small quantities in the refrigerator for up to 3 days.

Fresh Lamb Stock

MAKES 1.75 LITRES/3 PINTS

about 1 kg/2 lb 4 oz bones from
    a cooked joint or raw chopped
    lamb bones

2 onions, studded with 6 cloves, or
    sliced or chopped coarsely

2 carrots, sliced

1 leek, sliced

1–2 celery sticks, sliced

1 bouquet garni

about 2.25 litres/4 pints water

1 Chop or break up the bones and put into a large pan with the other ingredients.

2 Bring to the boil over a medium heat. Using a slotted spoon, skim away any scum on the surface. Reduce the heat to a gentle simmer, partially cover and cook for 3-4 hours. Strain the stock and leave to cool.

3 Remove any fat from the surface and chill in the refrigerator. If stored for more than 24 hours the stock must be boiled every day, cooled quickly and chilled. The stock may be frozen for up to 2 months; place in a large plastic bag and seal, leaving at least 2.5 cm/1 inch of headspace to allow for expansion.

Fresh Fish Stock

MAKES 1.75 LITRES/3 PINTS

1 head of a cod or salmon, etc. plus
    the trimmings, skin and bones or
    just the trimmings, skin and bones

1–2 onions, sliced

1 carrot, sliced

1–2 celery sticks, sliced

good squeeze of lemon juice

1 bouquet garni or 2 bay leaves

1 Wash the fish head and trimmings and put into a large pan. Cover with water and bring to the boil over a medium heat.

2 Using a slotted spoon, skim away any scum on the surface, then add the remaining ingredients. Reduce the heat, cover and simmer for 30 minutes. Strain and cool.

3 Store in the refrigerator and use within 2 days.

Italian Cheese Sauce

Melt 2 tbsp butter in a pan and stir in 25 g/1 oz plain flour until crumbly. Stir in 300 ml/10 fl oz hot milk until thick and smooth. Add a pinch of nutmeg, dried thyme, 2 tbsp white wine vinegar and season to taste with salt and pepper. Stir in 3 tbsp double cream, 55 g/2 oz each freshly grated mozzarella and Parmesan cheeses, 1 tsp English mustard and 2 tsp soured cream. Mix together.

Soups

Soups are an important part of the Italian cuisine. They vary in consistency from light and delicate to hearty main meal soups. Texture is always apparent – Italians rarely serve smooth soups. Some may be partially puréed but the identity of the ingredients is never entirely obliterated. There are regional characteristics, too. In the north, soups are often based on rice, while in Tuscany, thick bean- or bread-based soups are popular. Tomato, garlic and pasta soups are typical of the south. Minestrone is known world-wide but the best-known version probably comes from Milan. However, all varieties are full of vegetables and are delicious and satisfying. Fish soups also abound in one guise or another, and most of these are village specialities, so the variety is unlimited and always tasty.

minestrone soup

serves eight–ten

3 garlic cloves

3 large onions

2 celery sticks

2 large carrots

2 large potatoes

100 g/3½ oz French beans

100 g/3½ oz courgettes

55 g/2 oz butter

50 ml/2 fl oz olive oil

55 g/2 oz rindless fatty bacon,
    diced finely

1.5 litres/2¾ pints vegetable or
    chicken stock

1 bunch fresh basil, finely chopped

100 g/3½ oz chopped tomatoes

2 tbsp tomato purée

100 g/3½ oz Parmesan cheese rind

85 g/3 oz dried spaghetti,
    broken up

salt and pepper

freshly grated Parmesan cheese,
    to serve

1 Finely chop the garlic, onions, celery, carrots, potatoes, beans and courgettes with a sharp knife.

2 Heat the butter and oil together in a large pan over a medium heat. Add the bacon and fry for 2 minutes. Add the garlic and onion and fry for 2 minutes. Stir in the celery, carrots and potatoes and fry for 2 minutes.

3 Add the chopped beans to the pan and fry for 2 minutes. Stir in the courgettes and fry for a further 2 minutes. Cover the pan and cook all the vegetables, stirring frequently, for about 15 minutes.

4 Add the stock, basil, tomatoes, tomato purée and cheese rind. Season to taste with salt and pepper. Bring to the boil and simmer for 1 hour. Remove the cheese rind and discard.

5 Add the spaghetti to the pan and cook for 20 minutes.

6 Ladle the soup into large, warmed soup bowls, sprinkle with Parmesan cheese and serve.

COOK'S TIP

There are almost as many recipes for minestrone as there are cooks in Italy! You can add almost any vegetables you like and canned beans, such as flageolet.

bean & pasta soup

serves four

225 g/8 oz dried haricot beans,
   soaked, drained and rinsed

4 tbsp olive oil

2 large onions, sliced

3 garlic cloves, chopped

400 g/14 oz canned
   chopped tomatoes

1 tsp dried oregano

1 tsp tomato purée

850 ml/1½ pints water

85 g/3 oz dried pasta shapes

125 g/4½ oz sun-dried tomatoes,
   drained and sliced thinly

1 tbsp chopped fresh coriander or
   flat-leaf parsley

2 tbsp freshly grated
   Parmesan cheese

salt and pepper

1 Put the beans into a large pan, cover with cold water and bring to the boil. Boil rapidly for 10 minutes to remove any toxins. Drain and rinse.

2 Heat the oil in a large pan over a medium heat. Add the onions and fry until they are just starting to change colour. Stir in the garlic and cook for 1 further minute. Stir in the chopped tomatoes, oregano and the tomato purée. Pour over the water.

3 Add the cooked, drained beans to the mixture in the pan, bring to the boil and cover. Simmer for about 45 minutes, or until the beans are almost tender.

4 Add the pasta, season to taste with salt and pepper and stir in the sun-dried tomatoes. Return the soup to the boil, partially cover and continue cooking for 10 minutes, or until the pasta is nearly tender.

5 Stir in the chopped coriander or parsley. Taste the soup and adjust the seasoning, if necessary. Ladle the soup into 4 warmed soup bowls, sprinkle with the Parmesan cheese and serve immediately.

potato & parsley soup with pesto

serves four

3 slices rindless, smoked,
  fatty bacon
450 g/1 lb floury potatoes
450 g/ 1 lb onions
25 g/1 oz butter
600 ml/1 pint chicken stock
600 ml/1 pint milk
100 g/3½ oz dried conchigliette
150 ml/5 fl oz double cream
chopped fresh parsley
salt and pepper
PESTO SAUCE
55 g/2 oz chopped fresh parsley
2 garlic cloves, crushed
55 g/2 oz pine kernels, crushed
2 tbsp chopped fresh basil leaves
55 g/2 oz freshly grated
  Parmesan cheese
white pepper
150 ml/5 fl oz olive oil
TO SERVE
fresh Parmesan cheese shavings
garlic bread

1 To make the pesto sauce, put all the sauce ingredients into a food processor or blender and process for 2 minutes, or blend by hand.

2 Chop the bacon, potatoes and onions. Dry-fry the bacon in a pan over a medium heat for 4 minutes. Add the butter, potatoes and onions and cook for 12 minutes, stirring.

3 Add the stock and milk, bring to the boil over a medium heat and simmer for 10 minutes. Add the pasta and simmer for 12–14 minutes.

4 Blend in the cream and simmer for 5 minutes. Add the parsley and 2 tablespoons of pesto sauce. Ladle into 4 soup bowls and serve with the remaining pesto sauce, the Parmesan cheese and garlic bread.

italian fish soup

serves four

55 g/2 oz butter

450 g/1 lb assorted fish fillets, such
as red mullet and snapper

450 g/1 lb prepared seafood, such
as squid and prawns

225 g/8 oz fresh crabmeat

1 large onion, sliced

25 g/1 oz plain flour

1.2 litres/2 pints fish stock

100 g/3½ oz small, dried pasta
shapes, such as ditalini

1 tbsp anchovy essence

grated rind and juice of 1 orange

50 ml/2 fl oz dry sherry

300 ml/10 fl oz double cream

salt and pepper

grated orange rind, to garnish

3 Gradually add the stock, stirring,
until the soup comes to the boil.
Reduce the heat and simmer for about
30 minutes.

4 Add the pasta to the pan and
cook for a further 10 minutes.

5 Stir in the anchovy essence,
orange rind and juice, sherry and
the cream. Season to taste with salt
and pepper.

6 Heat the soup until completely
warmed through. Ladle the soup
into a large, warmed tureen or into
4 large, warmed soup bowls and
garnish with some grated orange rind.
Serve immediately.

1 Melt the butter in a large pan
over a low heat. Add the fish
fillets, seafood, crabmeat and onion
and cook gently for 6 minutes.

2 Add the flour to the mixture,
stirring carefully to avoid
any lumps.

chicken soup with stars

serves five–six

1.25 kg/2 lb 12 oz chicken pieces,
    such as wings or legs

2.5 litres/4½ pints water

1 celery stick, sliced

1 large carrot, sliced

1 onion, sliced

1 leek, sliced

2 garlic cloves, crushed

8 peppercorns

4 allspice berries

3–4 fresh parsley stems

2–3 fresh thyme sprigs

1 bay leaf

85 g/3 oz small, dried pasta stars or
    other very small shapes

salt and pepper

chopped fresh parsley, to garnish

1 Put the chicken into a large flameproof casserole dish with the water, celery, carrot, onion, leek, garlic, peppercorns, allspice, herbs and ½ teaspoon of salt. Bring just to the boil over a medium heat and skim off the foam that rises to the surface. Reduce the heat, partially cover and simmer for 2 hours.

2 Remove the chicken from the stock and leave to cool. Continue simmering the stock, uncovered, for about 30 minutes. When the chicken is cool enough to handle, remove the meat from the bones and, if necessary, cut into bite-sized pieces.

3 Strain the stock and remove as much fat as possible. Discard the vegetables and flavourings. (There should be about 1.7 litres/3 pints chicken stock.)

4 Bring the stock to the boil in a clean pan over a medium heat. Add the pasta and reduce the heat so the stock boils very gently. Cook for about 10 minutes, or until the pasta is tender, but still firm to the bite.

5 Stir in the chicken. Taste and adjust the seasoning. Ladle into bowls, sprinkle with parsley and serve.

15

prawn dumpling soup

serves four

DUMPLINGS

150 g/5½ oz plain flour

50 ml/2 fl oz boiling water

2 tbsp cold water

1½ tsp vegetable oil

FILLING

125 g/4½ oz minced pork

125 g/4½ oz cooked, peeled
    prawns, chopped

50 g/1¾ oz canned water chestnuts,
    drained, rinsed and chopped

1 celery stick, chopped

1 tsp cornflour

1 tbsp sesame oil

1 tbsp light soy sauce

SOUP

850 ml/1½ pints fish stock

50 g/1¾ oz cellophane noodles

1 tbsp dry sherry

snipped fresh chives, to garnish

1 To make the dumplings, mix the flour, boiling water, cold water and oil together in a bowl until a pliable dough is formed.

2 Knead the dough on a floured work surface for 5 minutes, then cut the dough into 16 equal-sized pieces.

3 Roll the dough pieces into rounds about 7.5 cm/3 inches in diameter.

4 Mix all the filling ingredients together in a large bowl.

5 Spoon a little of the filling mixture into the centre of each round. Bring the edges of the dough together, scrunching them up to form a 'moneybag' shape. Twist to seal.

6 Pour the fish stock into a pan and bring to the boil over a low heat.

7 Add the noodles, dumplings and sherry to the pan and cook for 4–5 minutes, or until the noodles and dumplings are tender. Ladle the soup into 4 warmed soup bowls, garnish with snipped chives and serve.

vermicelli & vegetable soup

serves four

1 small aubergine

2 large tomatoes

1 potato, peeled

1 carrot

1 leek

400 g/14 oz canned
cannellini beans

850 ml/1½ pints hot vegetable or
chicken stock

2 tsp dried basil

10 g/¼ oz dried porcini mushrooms,
soaked for 20 minutes in enough
almost boiling water to cover

50 g/1¾ oz dried vermicelli

3 tbsp Pesto (see page 13)

freshly grated Parmesan cheese, to
serve (optional)

3 Put the beans and their liquid
into a pan. Add the aubergine,
tomatoes, potatoes, carrot and leek. Stir.

4 Add the stock and bring to the
boil over a medium heat. Reduce
the heat and simmer for 15 minutes.

1 Slice the aubergine into rings
about 1-cm/½-inch thick, then cut
each ring into 4 pieces.

5 Add the basil, dried mushrooms,
their soaking liquid and the
vermicelli and simmer for 5 minutes or
until all of the vegetables are tender.

2 Cut the tomatoes and potato into
small dice. Cut the carrot into
sticks about 2.5-cm/1-inch long and
cut the leek into rings.

6 Remove the pan from the heat
and stir in the Pesto (see page 13).

7 Ladle the soup into 4 large,
warmed soup bowls and serve
with Parmesan cheese (if using).

noodle soup

serves four

3 slices smoked, rindless fatty
  bacon, diced
1 large onion, chopped
15 g/½ oz butter
450 g/1 lb dried peas, soaked
  in cold water for 2 hours
  and drained
2.3 litres/4 pints chicken stock
225 g/ 8 oz dried egg noodles
150 ml/5 fl oz double cream
salt and pepper
chopped fresh parsley, to garnish
Parmesan cheese croûtons (see
  Cook's Tip), to serve

1 Put the bacon, onion and butter into a large pan and cook over a low heat for about 6 minutes.

2 Add the peas and the stock to the pan and bring the mixture to the boil. Season lightly with salt and pepper, cover and simmer for about 1½ hours.

3 Add the egg noodles to the pan and simmer for a further 15 minutes.

4 Pour in the cream and blend thoroughly. Ladle into a warmed tureen, garnish with fresh parsley and top with Parmesan cheese croûtons (see Cook's Tip). Serve immediately.

COOK'S TIP

To make Parmesan cheese croûtons, cut a French stick into slices. Coat each slice with olive oil and sprinkle with Parmesan cheese. Cook under a preheated hot grill for about 30 seconds.

minestrone with pesto

serves six

175 g/6 oz dried cannellini beans,
  soaked overnight
2.5 litres/4½ pints water or
  vegetable stock
1 large onion, chopped
1 leek, trimmed and sliced thinly
2 celery sticks, sliced very thinly
2 carrots, chopped
3 tbsp olive oil
2 tomatoes, peeled and
  chopped roughly
1 courgette, trimmed and
  sliced thinly
2 potatoes, diced
85 g/3 oz dried elbow macaroni or
  other small macaroni
salt and pepper
4–6 tbsp freshly grated Parmesan
  cheese, to serve (optional)
PESTO
2 tbsp pine kernels
5 tbsp olive oil
2 bunches fresh basil, stems removed
4–6 garlic cloves, crushed
85 g/3 oz freshly grated pecorino or
  Parmesan cheese

1 Drain the soaked beans, rinse and put into a pan with the water or stock (avoid using a very salty stock, or the beans will become tough during cooking). Bring to the boil over a low heat, cover and simmer for 1 hour.

2 Add the onion, leek, celery, carrots and oil. Cover and simmer for 4–5 minutes.

3 Add the tomatoes, courgette, potatoes and macaroni. Season to taste with salt and pepper. Cover again and continue to simmer for about 30 minutes or until very tender.

4 To make the pesto, heat 1 tablespoon of the oil in a pan over a low heat. Add the pine kernels and fry until pale brown, then drain. Put the basil, nuts and garlic into a food processor or blender and process until well chopped. Alternatively, chop the basil finely by hand, then put into a mortar with the crushed garlic and pound with a pestle. Gradually add the remaining oil until smooth. Turn into a bowl, add the cheese and season to taste. Mix thoroughly.

5 Add 1½ tablespoons of the pesto to the soup and stir until it is well blended. Simmer for a further 5 minutes and adjust the seasoning, if necessary. Ladle into 6 large, warmed soup bowls, sprinkle with Parmesan cheese (if using) and serve with the remaining pesto.

minestrade lentiche

serves four

4 rashers streaky bacon, cut into
  small squares

1 onion, chopped

2 garlic cloves, crushed

2 celery sticks, chopped

50 g/1¾ oz dried farfalline or
  spaghetti broken into pieces

420 g/14½ oz canned brown
  lentils, drained

1.2 litres/2 pints hot ham or
  vegetable stock

2 tbsp chopped fresh mint

4 fresh mint sprigs, to garnish

1 Put the bacon into a large frying pan together with the onions, garlic and celery. Dry-fry for about 4–5 minutes over a low heat, stirring, until the onion is tender and the bacon is just starting to brown.

2 Add the farfalline or spaghetti pieces to the pan and cook, stirring, for about 1 minute to coat the pasta in the oil.

3 Add the lentils and stock. Bring to the boil over a medium heat, then reduce the heat and simmer until the pasta is tender.

4 Remove the pan from the heat and stir in the chopped mint.

5 Ladle the soup into 4 warmed soup bowls, garnish with a mint sprig and serve immediately.

VARIATION

Any type of pasta can be used in this recipe: try fusilli, conchiglie or rigatoni, if you prefer.

COOK'S TIP

If you prefer to use dried lentils, add the stock before the pasta and cook for 1–1¼ hours or until the lentils are tender. Add the pasta and cook for a further 12–15 minutes.

chicken & bean soup

serves four

2 tbsp butter

3 spring onions, chopped

2 garlic cloves, crushed

1 fresh marjoram sprig,
    chopped finely

350 g/12 oz boned chicken
    breasts, diced

1.2 litres/2 pints chicken stock

350 g/12 oz canned
    chickpeas, drained

1 bouquet garni

1 red pepper, diced

1 green pepper, diced

115 g/4 oz small dried pasta
    shapes, such as elbow macaroni

salt and white pepper

croûtons, to serve

1 Melt the butter in a large pan over a medium heat. Add the spring onions, garlic, marjoram sprig and diced chicken and cook, stirring frequently, for 5 minutes.

2 Add the chicken stock, chick peas and bouquet garni. Season to taste with salt and white pepper.

3 Bring the soup to the boil over a medium heat. Reduce the heat and simmer for about 2 hours.

4 Add the diced peppers and pasta shapes to the pan, then simmer for a further 20 minutes.

5 Ladle the soup into 4 warmed serving bowls and garnish with croûtons. Serve immediately.

chicken ravioli in tarragon broth

serves six

2 litres/3½ pints chicken stock

2 tbsp finely chopped fresh
   tarragon leaves

freshly grated Parmesan cheese,
   to serve

HOMEMADE PASTA DOUGH

125 g/4½ oz pasta or strong white
   flour, plus extra if needed

2 tbsp fresh tarragon leaves, with
   stems removed

1 egg

1 egg, separated

1 tsp extra virgin olive oil

2–3 tbsp water

RAVIOLI FILLING

200 g/7 oz cooked chicken,
   chopped coarsely

½ tsp grated lemon rind

2 tbsp chopped mixed fresh
   tarragon, chives and parsley

4 tbsp whipping cream

salt and pepper

1 To make the pasta, put the flour, tarragon and salt into a food processor and process. Beat the egg, egg yolk, oil and 2 tablespoons of the water together. With the machine still running, pour in the egg mixture and process until it forms a ball, leaving the sides of the bowl virtually clean. If the dough is crumbly, add the remaining water. If the dough is sticky, add 1–2 tablespoons of flour and process until a ball forms. Wrap in clingfilm and chill in the refrigerator for 30 minutes. Reserve the egg white.

2 To make the filling, put the chicken, lemon rind and mixed herbs into a food processor and season to taste with salt and pepper. Chop finely, by pulsing. Scrape into a bowl and stir in the cream. Taste and adjust the seasoning, if necessary.

3 Divide the pasta dough in half. Cover one half with a damp tea towel and roll the other half on a floured work surface as thinly as possible, less than 2 mm/¹⁄₁₆ inch. Cut out rectangles 10 x 5 cm/4 x 2 inches.

4 Put rounded teaspoons of filling on one half of the dough pieces. Brush around the edges with the reserved egg white and fold in half. Press the edges gently but firmly to seal. Arrange the ravioli in one layer on a baking sheet, dusted generously with flour. Repeat with the remaining dough. Leave to dry in a cool place for about 15 minutes or chill in the refrigerator for 1–2 hours.

5 Bring a large pan of lightly salted water to the boil over a medium heat. Drop in half the ravioli and cook for about 4–6 minutes, or until just tender. Drain on a clean tea towel while cooking the remainder.

6 Meanwhile, put the stock and tarragon into a large pan and bring to the boil over a medium heat, then reduce the heat to bubble gently. Cover and simmer for 15 minutes to infuse. Add the cooked ravioli to the stock and simmer for 5 minutes, or until heated through. Ladle into 6 large, warmed soup bowls and serve immediately with Parmesan cheese.

avgolemono

1.2 litres/2 pints chicken stock

100 g/3½ oz dried orzo or other
  small pasta shapes

2 large eggs

4 tbsp lemon juice

salt and pepper

finely chopped fresh flat-leaf parsley,
  to garnish

fresh bread or buns, to serve

1 Pour the stock into a large pan and bring to the boil over a medium heat. Add the pasta and cook for 8–10 minutes, or until the pasta is tender, but still firm to the bite.

2 Whisk the eggs in a spotlessly clean grease-free bowl for at least 30 seconds. Add the lemon juice and continue whisking for a further 30 seconds.

3 Reduce the heat under the pan of stock and pasta until the stock is not boiling.

4 Gradually add 4–5 tablespoons of the hot (not boiling) stock to the lemon and egg mixture, whisking constantly. Gradually add another 225 ml/8 fl oz of the stock, whisking to prevent the eggs curdling.

5 Gradually pour the lemon and egg mixture into the pan, whisking until the soup thickens slightly. Do not allow it to boil. Season to taste with salt and pepper.

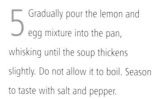

6 Ladle the soup into warmed soup bowls and sprinkle with the chopped parsley. Serve with bread.

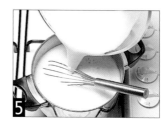

veal & wild mushroom soup

serves four

450 g/1 lb veal, sliced thinly

450 g/1 lb veal bones

1.2 litres/2 pints water

1 small onion

6 peppercorns

1 tsp cloves

pinch of mace

150 ml/5 fl oz double cream

140 g/5 oz oyster and shiitake
    mushrooms, chopped roughly

100 g/3½ oz dried vermicelli

1 tbsp cornflour

3 tbsp milk

salt and pepper

1 Put the veal, bones and water into a large pan and bring to the boil over a medium heat. Reduce the heat and add the onion, peppercorns, cloves and mace. Simmer for 3 hours until the stock is reduced by one-third.

2 Strain the stock into a clean pan, skim off any fat on the surface with a slotted spoon. Add the veal meat to the pan.

3 Add the cream and mushrooms to the pan and bring to the boil over a low heat. Simmer for 12 minutes, stirring occasionally.

4 Bring a large pan of lightly salted water to the boil over a medium heat. Add the vermicelli and cook for 10 minutes, or until tender, but still firm to the bite. Drain and keep warm.

5 Mix the cornflour and milk together to form a smooth paste and stir into the soup. Season to taste with salt and pepper and, just before serving, add the vermicelli. Ladle into 4 warmed soup bowls and serve.

beef & noodle soup

serves four

225 g/8 oz lean beef

1 garlic clove, crushed

2 spring onions, chopped

3 tbsp soy sauce

1 tsp sesame oil

225 g/8 oz dried egg noodles

850 ml/1½ pints beef stock

3 baby corn, sliced

½ leek, shredded

125 g/4½ oz broccoli, cut
   into florets

pinch of chilli powder

VARIATION

Vary the vegetables used or
use those to hand. If preferred,
use a few drops of chilli sauce
instead of chilli powder, but
remember it is very hot!

---

1 Cut the beef into thin strips with a
sharp knife and put into a bowl
with the garlic, spring onions, soy
sauce and sesame oil.

2 Mix the ingredients together in
the bowl, turning the beef to
coat. Cover and leave to marinate in
the refrigerator for 30 minutes.

3 Bring a pan of water to the boil
over a medium heat. Add the
noodles and cook for 3–4 minutes.
Drain thoroughly and reserve.

4 Put the stock into a large pan and
bring to the boil over a medium
heat. Add the beef, with the marinade,
baby corn, leek and broccoli. Cover
and simmer over a low heat for about
7–10 minutes, or until the beef and
vegetables are tender.

5 Stir in the cooked noodles and
chilli powder and cook for a
further 2–3 minutes.

6 Ladle the soup into 4 warmed
bowls and serve immediately.

italian fish stew

serves four

2 tbsp olive oil

2 red onions, chopped finely

1 garlic clove, crushed

2 courgettes, sliced

400 g/14 oz canned
    chopped tomatoes

850 ml/1½ pints fish or
    vegetable stock

85 g/3 oz small, dried pasta shapes

350 g/12 oz firm white fish, such
    as cod, haddock or hake

1 tbsp chopped fresh basil or
    oregano or 1 tsp dried oregano

1 tsp grated lemon rind

1 tbsp cornflour

1 tbsp water

salt and pepper

4 fresh basil or oregano sprigs,
    to garnish

1 Heat the oil in a large pan over a low heat. Add the onions and garlic and cook, stirring occasionally, for about 5 minutes until softened. Add the courgettes and cook, stirring frequently, for 2–3 minutes.

2 Add the tomatoes and stock to the pan and bring to the boil over a medium heat. Add the pasta, bring back to the boil, then reduce the heat and cover. Simmer for 5 minutes.

3 Skin and bone the fish, then cut it into chunks. Add to the pan with the basil or oregano and lemon rind and simmer gently for 5 minutes until the fish is opaque and flakes easily (take care not to overcook it) and the pasta is tender, but still firm to the bite.

4 Blend the cornflour with the water to form a smooth paste and stir into the stew. Cook for 2 minutes,

stirring constantly, until thickened. Season to taste with salt and pepper.

5 Ladle the stew into 4 large, warmed soup bowls. Garnish with fresh basil or oregano sprigs and serve immediately.

noodle & mushroom soup

serves four

15 g/½ oz dried Chinese
   mushrooms or 125 g/4½ oz field
   or chestnut mushrooms

1 litre/1¾ pints hot vegetable stock

125 g/4½ oz thread egg noodles

2 tsp sunflower oil

3 garlic cloves, crushed

2.5-cm/1-inch piece fresh root
   ginger, cut into fine shreds

½ tsp mushroom ketchup

1 tsp light soy sauce

125 g/4½ oz bean sprouts

fresh coriander leaves, to garnish

1 Soak the Chinese mushrooms (if
   using) for at least 30 minutes in
300 ml/10 fl oz of the stock. Remove
the stalks and discard, then slice the
mushrooms. Reserve the stock.

2 Bring a pan of water to the boil
   over a medium heat. Add the
noodles and cook for 2–3 minutes.
Drain well and rinse. Reserve.

3 Heat a wok over a high heat. Add
   the oil and when hot, add the
garlic and ginger. Stir and add the
mushrooms. Stir-fry for 2 minutes.

COOK'S TIP
Rice noodles contain no fat
and are ideal for for anyone on
a low-fat diet.

4 Add the remaining vegetable
   stock with the reserved stock and
bring to the boil over a medium heat.
Add the ketchup and soy sauce.

5 Stir in the bean sprouts and cook
   until tender. Put some noodles
into each serving bowl and ladle the
soup on top. Garnish with coriander
leaves and serve immediately.

mussel & potato soup

serves four

750 g/1 lb 10 oz mussels

2 tbsp olive oil

100 g/3½ oz unsalted butter

2 slices rindless, fatty
   bacon, chopped

1 onion, chopped

2 garlic cloves, crushed

55 g/2 oz plain flour

450 g/1 lb potatoes, sliced thinly

100 g/3½ oz dried conchigliette

300 ml/10 fl oz double cream

1 tbsp lemon juice

2 egg yolks

salt and pepper

2 tbsp finely chopped fresh parsley,
   to garnish

1 Pull off the 'beards' from the mussels and scrub them under cold water for 5 minutes. Discard any mussels that refuse to close when sharply tapped with a knife.

2 Bring a large pan of water to the boil over a medium heat. Add the mussels, oil and a little pepper and cook until the mussels open.

3 Drain the mussels, reserving the cooking liquid. Discard any mussels that have not opened. Remove the mussels from their shells.

4 Melt the butter in a pan over a low heat. Add the bacon, onion and garlic and cook for 4 minutes. Carefully stir in the flour. Measure 1.2 litres/2 pints of the reserved cooking liquid and stir into the pan.

5 Add the potatoes to the pan and simmer for 5 minutes. Add the pasta, then simmer for a further 10 minutes.

6 Add the cream and lemon juice, season to taste with salt and pepper, then add the mussels to the pan.

7 Blend the egg yolks with 1–2 tablespoons of the remaining cooking liquid, stir into the pan and cook for 4 minutes.

8 Ladle the soup into 4 warmed soup bowls and garnish with the chopped parsley. Serve immediately.

Light Meals

Recipes for snacks and light meals offer something for every taste, including vegetables, meat and fish dishes. These recipes are suitable for when you are not too hungry, but still a bit peckish, or if you are in a hurry and want to eat something quick, but still nutritious and tasty. Try the mouth-watering Italian flavours of Ravioli alla Parmigiana or even an Italian-style omelette – they are sure to satisfy even the most discerning taste buds. All of the recipes in this chapter are quick to prepare and easy to cook, and are sure to become staples in your Italian culinary repertoire.

ravioli alla parmigiana

serves four

280 g/10 oz Homemade Pasta
Dough made without fresh
tarragon (see page 24)

1 egg white, beaten lightly

1.2 litres/2 pints veal stock

freshly grated Parmesan cheese,
for sprinkling

RAVIOLI FILLING

100 g/3½ oz freshly grated
Parmesan cheese

100 g/3½ oz fine white
breadcrumbs

2 eggs

125 ml/4 fl oz Espagnole Sauce
(see Cook's Tip)

1 small onion, chopped finely

1 tsp freshly grated nutmeg

1 Make the Homemade Pasta
Dough (see page 24). Carefully
roll out 2 sheets of the pasta dough
and cover with a damp tea towel while
you make the filling for the ravioli.

2 To make the ravioli filling, using a
metal spoon, mix the Parmesan
cheese, breadcrumbs, eggs, Espagnole
Sauce (see Cook's Tip), chopped onion
and the grated nutmeg together in a
large mixing bowl.

3 Put spoonfuls of the filling at
regular intervals on to 1 sheet of
the dough. Cover with the second
sheet of dough, then cut into squares
and seal the edges with the egg white.

4 Bring the stock to the boil in a
large pan over a medium heat.
Add the ravioli to the pan and cook for
about 15 minutes.

5 Transfer the soup and ravioli to
4 warmed serving bowls, sprinkle
generously with Parmesan cheese and
serve immediately.

COOK'S TIP

For Espagnole Sauce, melt 2 tbsp
butter over a low heat and stir in
25 g/1 oz plain flour. Cook,
stirring, until lightly coloured.
Add 1 tsp tomato purée, then stir
in 425 ml/15 fl oz hot veal stock,
1 tbsp Madeira and 1½ tsp white
wine vinegar. Dice 25 g/1 oz
each bacon, carrot and onion
and 15 g/½ oz each celery, leek
and fennel. Fry with a fresh
thyme sprig and a bay leaf in
oil until soft. Drain, add to the
sauce and simmer for 2–3 hours.
Strain before using.

smoked ham linguini

serves four

450 g/1 lb dried linguine

450 g/1 lb broccoli florets

150 ml/5 fl oz Italian Cheese Sauce
  (see page 7)

225 g/8 oz Italian smoked ham

salt and pepper

1 Bring a large pan of lightly salted water to the boil over a medium heat. Add the pasta and broccoli and cook for 10 minutes, or until the pasta is tender, but still firm to the bite.

2 Drain the pasta and broccoli thoroughly, then reserve and keep warm.

3 Meanwhile, make the Italian Cheese Sauce (see page 7).

4 Cut the Italian smoked ham into thin strips. Toss the pasta, broccoli and ham into the Italian Cheese Sauce, then gently warm through over a very low heat.

5 Transfer the pasta mixture to a large, warmed serving dish. Sprinkle with pepper and serve.

creamed veal kidneys with pesto sauce

serves four

75 g/2¾ oz butter

12 veal kidneys, trimmed and
   sliced thinly

175 g/6 oz button
   mushrooms, sliced

1 tsp English mustard

pinch of freshly grated root ginger

2 tbsp dry sherry

150 ml/5 fl oz double cream

2 tbsp Pesto Sauce (see page 13)

400 g/14 oz dried penne

salt and pepper

4 slices of hot toast, cut
   into triangles

4 fresh parsley sprigs, to garnish

1 Melt the butter in a frying pan over a low heat. Add the kidneys and fry for 4 minutes. Transfer to an ovenproof dish and keep warm.

2 Add the sliced mushrooms to the frying pan and cook for about 2 minutes.

3 Add the mustard and ginger to the pan. Season to taste with salt and pepper. Cook for 2 minutes, then add the sherry, cream and Pesto Sauce (see page 13). Cook for 3 minutes, then pour over the kidneys. Bake in a preheated oven at 190°C/375°F/Gas Mark 5 for 10 minutes.

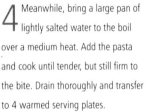

4 Meanwhile, bring a large pan of lightly salted water to the boil over a medium heat. Add the pasta and cook until tender, but still firm to the bite. Drain thoroughly and transfer to 4 warmed serving plates.

5 Top the pasta with the kidneys in the Pesto Sauce. Put triangles of warm toast around the kidneys, garnish with fresh parsley sprigs and serve immediately.

chicken scallops

serves four

175 g/6 oz dried short-cut macaroni,
    or other short pasta shapes
2 tbsp vegetable oil, plus extra
    for brushing
1 onion, chopped finely
3 rashers unsmoked collar or back
    bacon, derinded and chopped
125 g/4¼ oz button mushrooms,
    sliced thinly or chopped
175 g/6 oz cooked chicken, diced
175 ml/6 fl oz crème fraîche
4 tbsp dry breadcrumbs
75 g/2¼ oz freshly grated
    Cheddar cheese
salt and pepper
fresh flat-leaf parsley sprigs, to garnish

1 Bring a large pan of lightly salted water to the boil over a medium heat. Add the pasta and cook for about 8–10 minutes, or until tender, but still firm the the bite. Drain well, return to the pan and cover.

2 Heat the remaining oil in a frying pan over a medium heat. Add the onion and fry until translucent. Add the bacon and mushrooms and cook for 3–4 minutes, stirring once or twice.

3 Stir in the cooked pasta, chicken and crème fraîche and season to taste with salt and pepper.

4 Brush 4 large scallop shells with oil. Spoon in the chicken mixture and smooth with a wooden spoon to make neat mounds.

5 Mix the breadcrumbs and cheese together, and sprinkle over the top of the shells. Press the topping into the chicken mixture and cook under a preheated hot grill for 4–5 minutes, until golden and bubbling. Garnish with fresh parsley sprigs and serve hot.

chorizo & wild mushrooms

serves six

650 g/1 lb 7 oz dried vermicelli

125 ml/4 fl oz olive oil

2 garlic cloves, chopped finely

125 g/4½ oz chorizo, sliced

225 g/8 oz wild mushrooms, sliced

1–3 fresh red chillies, chopped

salt and pepper

TO GARNISH

2 tbsp Parmesan cheese shavings

10 anchovy fillets

COOK'S TIP

Always obtain wild mushrooms from a reliable source and never pick them yourself unless you are absolutely certain of their identity. Oyster mushrooms of mixed colours have been used here, but you could also use chanterelles.

1 Bring a large pan of lightly salted water to the boil over a medium heat. Add the pasta and cook until tender, but still firm to the bite. Drain thoroughly and put into a large warmed serving dish. Keep warm.

2 Meanwhile, heat the the oil in a large frying pan over a low heat. Add the garlic and fry for 1 minute. Add the chorizo and the mushrooms and cook for 4 minutes, then add the chillies and cook for 1 further minute to mix the flavours.

3 Pour the chorizo and mushroom mixture over the vermicelli and season to taste with a little salt and pepper. Transfer to 4 warmed serving plates and garnish with shavings of Parmesan cheese and a decorative lattice of anchovy fillets. Serve.

olive, pepper & cherry tomato pasta

serves four

225 g/8 oz dried orecchiette

2 tbsp olive oil

2 tbsp butter

2 garlic cloves, crushed

1 green pepper, sliced thinly

1 yellow pepper, sliced thinly

16 cherry tomatoes, halved

1 tbsp chopped fresh oregano

125 ml/4 fl oz dry white wine

2 tbsp quartered black olives

75 g/2¾ oz rocket leaves

salt and pepper

TO GARNISH

fresh Parmesan cheese shavings

1 fresh oregano sprig

COOK'S TIP

Ensure that the pan is large enough to prevent the pasta strands from sticking together during cooking.

2 Heat the oil and butter in a large frying pan over a low heat. Add the garlic and fry for 30 seconds. Add the peppers and cook for 3–4 minutes, stirring constantly.

3 Stir in the cherry tomatoes, oregano, wine and olives and cook for 3–4 minutes. Season well with salt and pepper and stir in the rocket until just wilted.

1 Bring a pan of lightly salted water to the boil over a medium heat. Add the pasta and cook until tender, but still firm to the bite. Drain.

4 Transfer the pasta to a serving dish, spoon over the sauce and mix well. Garnish with the Parmesan cheese and an oregano sprig. Serve.

spaghetti alla carbonara

serves four

425 g/15 oz dried spaghetti

1 tbsp olive oil

1 large onion, sliced thinly

2 garlic cloves, chopped

175 g/6 oz rindless bacon, cut into
   thin strips

25 g/1 oz butter

175 g/6 oz mushrooms, sliced thinly

300 ml/10 fl oz double cream

3 eggs, beaten

100 g/3½ oz freshly grated
   Parmesan cheese, plus extra to
   serve (optional)

salt and pepper

fresh sage sprigs, to garnish

COOK'S TIP

The key to success with this recipe is not to overcook the egg. That is why it is important to keep all the ingredients hot enough just to cook the egg, then work rapidly to avoid it scrambling.

1 Bring a large pan of lightly salted water to the boil over a medium heat. Add the pasta and cook until tender, but still firm to the bite. Drain well, return to the pan and keep warm.

2 Meanwhile, heat the oil in a large frying pan over a medium heat. Add the onion and fry until it is translucent. Add the garlic and bacon and fry until the bacon is crisp. Transfer to a warmed plate.

3 Melt the butter in the frying pan over a medium heat. Add the mushrooms and fry for 3–4 minutes, then return the bacon mixture to the pan. Cover and keep warm.

4 Whisk the cream, eggs and cheese together in a large bowl, then season with salt and pepper.

5 Working very quickly, tip the pasta into the bacon and mushroom mixture and pour over the eggs. Using 2 forks, toss the pasta into the egg and cream mixture and season with pepper to taste. Garnish with fresh sage sprigs and serve with extra grated Parmesan cheese, if you wish.

tricolour timballini

serves four

1 tbsp butter, softened

55 g/2 oz dry white breadcrumbs

175 g/6 oz dried tricoloured
spaghetti, broken into
5-cm/2-inch lengths

1 egg yolk

115 g/4 oz freshly grated
Gruyère cheese

300 ml/10 fl oz Béchamel Sauce
(see page 98)

2 tbsp olive oil

1 onion, chopped finely

1 bay leaf

150 ml/5 fl oz dry white wine

150 ml/5 fl oz passata

1 tbsp tomato purée

salt and pepper

1 Grease four 175-ml/6-fl oz
moulds or ramekin dishes with
the butter. Evenly coat the insides with
half the breadcrumbs.

2 Bring a pan of lightly salted water
to the boil over a medium heat.
Add the pasta and cook for about
8–10 minutes, or until just tender, but
still firm to the bite. Drain and transfer
to a bowl. Add the egg yolk and
cheese and mix well. Season to taste
with salt and pepper.

3 Stir the Béchamel Sauce (see page
98) into the pasta and mix well.
Spoon the pasta mixture into the
prepared moulds and sprinkle the
remaining breadcrumbs over the top.

4 Stand the moulds on a baking
sheet and bake in a preheated
oven at 220°C/425°F/Gas Mark 7, for
20 minutes. Remove from the oven
and leave for 10 minutes.

5 Meanwhile, make the sauce. Heat
the oil in a pan over a low heat.
Add the onion and bay leaf and cook
for 2–3 minutes. Stir in the wine,
passata and tomato purée and season
to taste. Simmer for about 20 minutes
until thickened. Remove the bay leaf
and discard.

6 Turn the timballini out on to
4 large, warmed serving plates
and serve immediately with the sauce.

pasta omelette

serves two

4 tbsp olive oil

1 small onion, chopped

1 fennel bulb, sliced thinly

115 g/4 oz potato, peeled and diced

1 garlic clove, chopped

4 eggs

1 tbsp chopped fresh
   flat-leaf parsley

pinch of chilli powder

100 g/3½ oz cooked short pasta

2 tbsp stuffed green olives, halved

salt and pepper

fresh marjoram sprigs, to garnish

tomato salad, to serve

1 Heat half the oil in a large frying pan over a low heat. Add the onion, fennel and potato and cook, stirring occasionally, for 8–10 minutes, or until the potato is just tender.

2 Stir in the garlic and cook for 1 minute. Remove the pan from the heat, transfer the vegetables to a plate and reserve.

3 Beat the eggs until frothy. Stir in the parsley and season with salt, pepper and a pinch of chilli powder.

4 Heat 1 tablespoon of the remaining oil in a clean frying pan. Add half the egg mixture to the pan, then add the cooked vegetables, pasta and half the olives. Pour in the remaining egg mixture and cook until the sides start to set.

5 Lift up the edges of the omelette with a palette knife to allow the uncooked egg to spread underneath. Cook until the underside is a light golden brown colour.

6 Slide the omelette out of the pan on to a plate. Wipe the pan with kitchen paper and heat the remaining oil. Invert the omelette into the pan and cook until the other side is golden.

7 Slide the omelette on to a large, warmed serving dish and garnish with the remaining olives and the fresh marjoram sprigs. Cut into wedges and serve with a tomato salad.

spaghetti with ricotta cheese sauce

serves four

350 g/12 oz dried spaghetti

3 tbsp butter

2 tbsp chopped fresh
flat-leaf parsley

fresh flat-leaf parsley sprigs,
to garnish

SAUCE

115 g/4 oz freshly ground almonds

115 g/4 oz ricotta cheese

pinch of freshly grated nutmeg

pinch of ground cinnamon

150 ml/5 fl oz crème fraîche

2 tbsp olive oil

125 ml/4 fl oz hot chicken stock

1 tbsp pine kernels

salt and pepper

COOK'S TIP

Use 2 large forks to toss
spaghetti or other long pasta, so
it is thoroughly coated with the
sauce. Specially designed
spaghetti forks are available from
some cookware departments and
large kitchen shops.

1 Bring a large pan of lightly salted
water to the boil over a medium
heat. Add the pasta and cook for about
8–10 minutes, or until tender, but still
firm to the bite.

2 Drain the pasta well, return to the
pan and toss with the butter and
chopped fresh parsley. Cover the pan
and keep warm.

3 To make the sauce, mix the
ground almonds, ricotta cheese,
nutmeg, cinnamon and crème fraîche
together in a small pan and stir over a
low heat until a thick paste forms.
Gradually stir in the oil. When the oil
has been fully incorporated, gradually
stir in the hot stock until smooth.
Season with pepper to taste.

4 Transfer the pasta to a large,
warmed serving dish, pour the
sauce over and toss together well with
2 forks (see Cook's Tip). Sprinkle over
the pine kernels, garnish with fresh
parsley sprigs and serve immediately.

tagliatelle with garlic butter

serves four

450 g/1 lb strong white flour, plus
  extra for dredging

2 tsp salt

4 eggs, beaten

2 tbsp olive oil

75 g/2¾ oz butter, melted

3 garlic cloves, chopped finely

2 tbsp chopped fresh parsley

pepper

1 Sift the flour into a large bowl and stir in the salt.

2 Make a well in the centre of the dry ingredients and add the eggs and oil. Using a wooden spoon, stir in the eggs, gradually drawing in the flour. After a few minutes the dough will be too stiff to use a spoon and you will need to use your fingers.

3 Turn the dough out on to a lightly floured work surface and knead for about 5 minutes or until smooth and elastic. If you find the dough is too wet, add a little more flour and continue kneading. Cover with cling film and chill in the refrigerator for 30 minutes. This makes the dough easier to roll and less likely to tear.

4 Roll out the pasta dough thinly and create the pasta shapes required. This can be done by hand or using a pasta machine. Results from a machine are usually neater and thinner, but not necessarily better.

5 To make the tagliatelle by hand, fold the thinly rolled pasta sheets into 3 and cut out long, thin strips, about 1-cm/½-inch wide.

6 Bring a large pan of water to the boil over a medium heat. Add the pasta and cook for 2–3 minutes, or until tender, but still firm to the bite. Drain and return the pasta to the pan.

7 Mix the butter, garlic and parsley together in a small bowl. Stir into the pasta, season with a little pepper to taste and serve immediately.

tagliarini with gorgonzola

serves four

25 g/1 oz butter

225 g/8 oz Gorgonzola cheese, crumbled roughly

150 ml/5 fl oz double cream

2 tbsp dry white wine

1 tsp cornflour

4 fresh sage sprigs, chopped finely

400 g/14 oz dried tagliarini

2 tbsp olive oil

salt and white pepper

1 fresh sage sprig, to garnish

1 Melt the butter in a pan over a low heat. Stir in 175 g/6 oz of the Gorgonzola cheese and melt for about 2 minutes.

2 Add the cream, wine and the cornflour to the pan and beat with a wooden spoon until blended.

3 Stir in the sage and season to taste with salt and white pepper. Bring to the boil over a low heat, beating constantly, until the sauce thickens. Remove from the heat and reserve while you cook the pasta.

4 Bring a large pan of lightly salted water to the boil over a medium heat. Add the pasta and cook for 12–14 minutes, or until just tender, but still firm to the bite. Drain well and toss in the oil. Transfer to a warmed serving dish and keep warm.

5 Return the pan containing the sauce to a low heat and warm through, beating constantly. Spoon the Gorgonzola sauce over the pasta, garnish with a fresh sage sprig and sprinkle over the remaining cheese. Serve immediately.

COOK'S TIP

Gorgonzola is one of the world's oldest veined cheeses. When buying, check that it is creamy yellow with green veining. Avoid hard or discoloured cheese. It should have a rich, piquant aroma, not a bitter smell.

fettuccine all' alfredo

serves four

2 tbsp butter

200 ml/7 fl oz double cream

450 g/1 lb fresh fettuccine

85 g/3 oz freshly grated Parmesan
cheese, plus extra to serve

pinch of freshly grated nutmeg

salt and pepper

1 fresh flat-leaf parsley sprig,
to garnish

VARIATION

This classic dish is often served
with the addition of ham and
peas. Add 225 g/8 oz shelled
cooked peas and 175 g/6 oz ham
strips with the cheese in step 4.

1 Put the butter and 150 ml/5 fl oz
of the cream into a large pan and
bring the mixture to the boil over
a medium heat. Reduce the heat, then
simmer gently for 1½ minutes, or until
the cream has thickened slightly.

2 Meanwhile, bring a large pan of
lightly salted water to the boil
over a medium heat. Add the pasta
and cook for 2–3 minutes, or until
tender, but still firm to the bite. Drain
thoroughly and return to the pan, then
pour over the cream sauce.

3 Toss the pasta in the sauce over a
low heat, stirring with a wooden
spoon, until coated thoroughly.

4 Add the remaining cream,
Parmesan cheese and nutmeg to
the pasta mixture and season to taste
with salt and pepper. Toss the pasta in
the mixture while heating through.

5 Transfer the pasta mixture to
a warmed serving plate and
garnish with the fresh parsley sprig.
Serve immediately with extra grated
Parmesan cheese.

rotelle with spicy italian sauce

serves four

200 ml/7 fl oz Italian Red Wine
  Sauce (see page 96)
4 tbsp olive oil
3 garlic cloves, crushed
2 fresh red chillies, chopped
1 fresh green chilli, chopped
400 g/14 oz dried rotelle
salt and pepper

1 Make the Italian Red Wine Sauce (see page 96).

2 Heat 4 tablespoons of the oil in a pan over a low heat. Add the garlic and chillies and fry for 3 minutes.

3 Stir in the Italian Red Wine Sauce, season to taste with salt and pepper and simmer gently over a low heat for 20 minutes.

4 Bring a large pan of lightly salted water to the boil over a medium heat. Add the pasta and cook for about 8 minutes, or until tender, but still firm to the bite. Drain thoroughly.

5 Toss the pasta in the spicy sauce, transfer to a warmed serving dish and serve immediately.

spaghetti olio e aglio

serves four

125 ml/4 fl oz olive oil

3 garlic cloves, crushed

450 g/1 lb fresh spaghetti

3 tbsp roughly chopped
   fresh parsley

salt and pepper

1 Heat the oil in a large pan over a low heat. Add the garlic and a pinch of salt and cook, stirring constantly, until golden brown, then remove the pan from the heat. Do not allow the garlic to burn as it will taint the flavour of the oil. (If it does burn, you will have to start all over again.)

2 Meanwhile, bring a large pan of lightly salted water to the boil over a medium heat. Add the pasta and cook for about 2–3 minutes, or until tender, but still firm to the bite.

Drain the pasta thoroughly and return to the pan. Keep warm.

3 Add the oil and garlic mixture to the pasta and toss to coat thoroughly. Season with pepper to taste, add the chopped parsley and toss to coat again.

4 Transfer the pasta to a large, warmed serving dish and serve.

penne with muscoli fritti nell' olio

serves four–six

400 g/14 oz dried penne

450 g/1 lb mussels, cooked
   and shelled

1 tsp sea salt

85 g/3 oz plain flour

125 ml/4 fl oz olive oil

100 g/3½ oz sun-dried
   tomatoes, sliced

2 tbsp chopped fresh basil

salt and pepper

TO GARNISH

1 lemon, sliced thinly

fresh basil sprigs

VARIATION

You could substitute clams for
the mussels. If using fresh clams,
try the smaller varieties, such
as Venus.

1 Bring a large pan of lightly salted water to the boil over a medium heat. Add the pasta and cook for about 8 minutes or until the pasta is just tender, but still firm to the bite.

2 Drain the pasta well and put into a large, warmed serving dish. Reserve and keep warm while you cook the mussels.

3 Lightly sprinkle the mussels with the sea salt. Season the flour with salt and pepper to taste, sprinkle into a bowl and toss the mussels in the flour until coated.

4 Heat the oil in a large frying pan over a medium heat: Add the mussels and fry, stirring frequently, until golden brown.

5 Toss the mussels with the reserved pasta and sprinkle with the sun-dried tomatoes and basil. Transfer to large plates and garnish with lemon slices and basil. Serve.

COOK'S TIP

Sun-dried tomatoes have been used in Mediterranean countries for a long time, but have become popular elsewhere only quite recently. They are dried and often preserved in oil. They have a concentrated, almost roasted flavour and a dense texture. They should be drained and chopped or sliced before using.

spicy tomato tagliatelle

serves four

50 g/1¾ oz butter

1 onion, chopped finely

1 garlic clove, crushed

2 small fresh red chillies, deseeded
    and diced

450 g/1 lb tomatoes, peeled,
    deseeded and diced

200 ml/7 fl oz vegetable stock

2 tbsp tomato purée

1 tsp sugar

675 g/1 lb 8 oz fresh green
    and white tagliatelle, or
    350 g/12 oz dried tagliatelle

salt and pepper

1 Melt the butter in a large frying pan over a medium-low heat. Add the onion and garlic and cook for 3–4 minutes or until softened.

2 Add the chillies to the pan and continue cooking for about 2 minutes.

3 Add the tomatoes and stock, then reduce the heat and simmer for 10 minutes, stirring constantly.

4 Pour the sauce into a food processor and process for about 1 minute or until smooth. Alternatively, rub the sauce through a sieve.

5 Return the sauce to the pan, add the tomato purée, sugar and salt and pepper to taste. Gently heat over a low heat until piping hot.

6 Bring a large pan of lightly salted water to the boil over a medium heat. Add the pasta and cook until tender, but still firm to the bite. Drain. Transfer to 4 warmed serving plates and serve tossed in the tomato sauce.

pasta with cheese & broccoli

serves four

300 g/10½ oz dried
   tricolour tagliatelle
225 g/8 oz broccoli, broken into
   small florets
350 g/12 oz mascarpone cheese
125 g/4½ oz blue cheese, chopped
1 tbsp chopped fresh oregano
25 g/1 oz butter
salt and pepper
4 fresh oregano sprigs, to garnish
freshly grated Parmesan cheese,
   to serve

1 Bring a large pan of lightly salted water to the boil over a medium heat. Add the pasta and cook until tender, but still firm to the bite.

2 Bring a pan of salted water to the boil over a low heat. Add the broccoli and cook. Avoid overcooking, so it retains its colour and texture.

3 Heat the mascarpone and blue cheeses together in a large pan over a very low heat until melted. Stir in the chopped oregano and season to taste with salt and pepper.

4 Drain the pasta thoroughly and return to the pan. Add the butter and toss the pasta until well coated. Drain the broccoli thoroughly and add it to the pasta with the sauce, tossing gently to mix.

5 Transfer the pasta to 4 large, warmed serving plates and garnish with fresh oregano sprigs. Serve with Parmesan cheese.

penne & butternut squash

serves four

2 tbsp olive oil

1 garlic clove, crushed

55 g/2 oz fresh white breadcrumbs

500 g/1 lb 2 oz butternut squash,
   peeled and deseeded

8 tbsp water

500 g/1 lb 2 oz fresh penne

1 tbsp butter

1 onion, sliced

115 g/4 oz ham, cut into strips

200 ml/7 fl oz single cream

55 g/2 oz freshly grated
   Cheddar cheese

2 tbsp chopped fresh parsley

salt and pepper

COOK'S TIP

If the squash weighs more than
is needed for this recipe, blanch
the excess for 3–4 minutes on
HIGH in a covered bowl with a
little water. Drain, cool and place
in a freezer bag. Store in the
freezer for up to 3 months.

1 Mix the oil, garlic and breadcrumbs together and spread out on a large plate. Cook in the microwave on HIGH for 4–5 minutes, stirring every minute, until crisp and starting to brown. Remove from the microwave and reserve.

2 Dice the squash and put into a large bowl with half the water. Cover and cook on HIGH for about 8–9 minutes, stirring occasionally. Leave to stand for 2 minutes.

3 Put the pasta into a large bowl, add a little salt and pour over enough boiling water to cover by 2.5 cm/1 inch. Cover and cook on HIGH for 5 minutes, stirring once, until the pasta is just tender, but still firm to the bite. Leave to stand, covered, for 1 minute before draining.

4 Put the butter and onion into a large bowl. Cover and cook on HIGH for 3 minutes.

5 Using a fork, coarsely mash the squash. Add to the onion with the pasta, ham, cream, cheese, parsley and remaining water. Season generously with salt and pepper and mix well. Cover and cook on HIGH for 4 minutes until heated through.

6 Transfer the pasta to 4 large, warmed serving plates and serve sprinkled with the crisp garlic crumbs.

pasta with basil & pine nut pesto

serves four

about 40 fresh basil leaves

3 garlic cloves, crushed

25 g/1 oz pine kernels

50 g/1¾ oz finely grated
   Parmesan cheese

2–3 tbsp extra virgin olive oil

675 g/1 lb 8 oz fresh pasta or
   350 g/12 oz dried pasta

salt and pepper

1 Rinse the basil leaves and pat dry on kitchen paper.

2 Put the basil leaves, garlic, pine kernels and grated Parmesan cheese into a food processor and process for 30 seconds or until smooth. Alternatively, put the ingredients in a mortar and pound with a pestle.

3 If using a food processor, keep the motor running and slowly add the oil. Alternatively, add the oil drop by drop while stirring briskly. Season to taste with salt and pepper.

4 Meanwhile, bring a large pan of lightly salted water to the boil over a medium heat. Add the pasta and cook until tender, but still firm to the bite. Drain thoroughly.

5 Transfer the pasta to a serving plate and serve with the pesto. Toss to mix well and serve hot.

fettuccine with walnut sauce

serves four–six

2 thick slices wholemeal bread,
    crusts removed
300 ml/10 fl oz milk
275 g/9½ oz shelled walnuts
2 garlic cloves, crushed
115 g/4 oz stoned black olives
55 g/2 oz freshly grated
    Parmesan cheese
8 tbsp extra virgin olive oil
150 ml/5 fl oz double cream
450 g/1 lb fresh fettuccine
2–3 tbsp chopped fresh parsley
salt and pepper

1. Put the slices of bread into a large shallow dish, pour over the milk and leave to soak until all the liquid has been absorbed.

2. Spread the walnuts out on a large baking tray and toast in a preheated oven at 190°C/375°F/Gas Mark 5, for about 5 minutes or until golden. Leave to cool.

3. Put the bread, walnuts, garlic, olives, Parmesan cheese and 6 tablespoons of the oil into a food processor and process until a smooth purée forms. Season to taste with salt and pepper, then stir in the cream.

4. Bring a large pan of lightly salted water to the boil over a medium heat. Add the pasta and cook for about 2–3 minutes, or until tender, but still firm to the bite. Drain thoroughly and toss with the remaining oil.

5. Transfer the pasta to 4 large, warmed serving plates and spoon the walnut sauce over the top. Sprinkle over the chopped parsley and serve.

spaghetti with smoked salmon

serves four

450 g/1 lb dried
  buckwheat spaghetti
1 tbsp olive oil
300 ml/10 fl oz double cream
150 ml/5 fl oz whisky or brandy
125 g/4½ oz smoked salmon
pinch of cayenne pepper
2 tbsp chopped fresh coriander
  or parsley
85 g/3 oz feta cheese, crumbled
  (drained weight)
salt and pepper
fresh coriander or parsley sprigs,
  to garnish

COOK'S TIP

Serve this rich and luxurious dish
with a green salad tossed in a
lemony dressing.

1 Bring a large pan of lightly salted water to the boil over a medium heat. Add the pasta and cook until tender, but still firm to the bite. Drain well, return the pasta to the pan and sprinkle over the oil. Cover, shake the pan, reserve and keep warm.

2 Pour the cream into a small pan and bring to simmering point, but do not allow it to boil. Pour the whisky or brandy into another small pan and bring to simmering point, but do not allow it to boil. Remove both pans from the heat and mix the cream and whisky or brandy together.

3 Cut the smoked salmon into thin strips and add to the cream mixture. Season to taste with cayenne and pepper. Just before serving, stir in the chopped fresh coriander or parsley.

4 Transfer the pasta to a warmed serving dish. Pour over the sauce and toss thoroughly with 2 large forks, then transfer to 4 warmed plates, scatter over the feta cheese and garnish with coriander sprigs. Serve.

pasta & sicilian sauce

serves four

450 g/1 lb tomatoes, halved

25 g/1 oz pine kernels

50 g/1¾ oz sultanas

50 g/1¾ oz canned anchovy fillets,
   drained and halved lengthways

2 tbsp concentrated tomato purée

675 g/1 lb 8 oz fresh penne or
   350 g/12 oz dried penne

COOK'S TIP

If you are making fresh pasta,
remember that pasta dough
prefers warm conditions and
responds well to handling. Do
not leave to chill and do not use
a marble surface for kneading.

1 Put the tomatoes under a preheated medium-hot grill and cook for 10 minutes. Leave until cool enough to handle, then peel off the skin and dice the flesh.

2 Put the pine kernels on to a baking tray and toast under the grill for 2–3 minutes or until golden.

3 Put the sultanas into a bowl and pour over enough warm water to cover. Leave to soak for 20 minutes, then drain well.

4 Put the tomatoes, pine kernels and sultanas into a pan and heat.

5 Add the anchovies and tomato purée, heating the sauce for a further 2–3 minutes or until hot.

6 Bring a pan of lightly salted water to the boil over a medium heat. Add the pasta and cook until tender, but still firm to the bite. Drain well.

7 Transfer the pasta to 4 large, warmed serving plates and serve with the hot Sicilian sauce.

baked rigatoni filled with tuna & ricotta

serves four

1 tbsp butter for greasing

450 g/1 lb dried rigatoni

1 tbsp olive oil

200 g/7 oz canned flaked
tuna, drained

225 g/8 oz ricotta cheese

125 ml/4 fl oz double cream

225 g/8 oz freshly grated
Parmesan cheese

125 g/4½ oz sun-dried tomatoes,
drained and sliced

salt and pepper

1 Lightly grease a large ovenproof
dish with the butter.

2 Bring a large pan of lightly salted
water to the boil over a medium
heat. Add the pasta and oil and cook
for 8–10 minutes, or until tender, but
still firm to the bite. Drain well, then
rinse in cold water and leave until cool
enough to handle.

3 Mix the tuna and ricotta cheese
together until blended to a soft
paste. Spoon into a piping bag and use
to fill the pasta. Arrange side by side in
a single layer in the prepared dish.

4 Mix the cream and the grated
Parmesan cheese together.
Season to taste with salt and pepper,
then spoon the mixture over the filled
pasta tubes in the dish.

5 Top with the sun-dried tomatoes,
arranged in a criss-cross pattern
and bake in a preheated oven at
200°C/400°F/Gas Mark 6, for about
20 minutes. Serve immediately.

fettuccine with anchovy & spinach sauce

serves four

900 g/2 lb fresh, young
  spinach leaves

400 g/14 oz dried fettuccine

5 tbsp olive oil

3 tbsp pine kernels

3 garlic cloves, crushed

8 canned anchovy fillets, drained
  and chopped

salt

COOK'S TIP

If you are in a hurry, you can
use frozen spinach. Thaw and
drain it thoroughly, pressing out
as much moisture as possible.
Cut the leaves into strips and
add to the dish with the
anchovies in step 4.

1 Trim off any tough spinach stalks. Rinse the spinach leaves and put them in a large pan with only the water that is clinging to them after washing. Cover and cook over a high heat, shaking the pan from time to time, until the spinach has wilted, but retains its colour. Drain well, reserve and keep warm.

2 Bring a large pan of lightly salted water to the boil over a medium heat. Add the pasta and cook for about 8–10 minutes, or until just tender, but still firm to the bite.

3 Meanwhile, heat 4 tablespoons of the oil in a small pan. Add the pine kernels and fry until just golden. Remove the pine kernels from the pan and reserve.

4 Add the garlic to the pan and fry until golden brown. Add the anchovies and stir in the wilted spinach. Cook, stirring, for about 2–3 minutes, or until heated through. Return the pine kernels to the pan.

5 Drain the pasta, toss in the remaining oil and transfer to a large, warmed serving dish. Spoon the anchovy and spinach sauce over the pasta and toss lightly, then transfer to 4 warmed serving plates and serve.

spaghetti with tuna & parsley sauce

serves four

500 g/1 lb 2 oz dried spaghetti

25 g/1 oz butter

4 fresh parsley sprigs, to garnish

SAUCE

200 g/7 oz canned tuna, drained

55 g/2 oz canned anchovy
   fillets, drained

250 ml/9 fl oz olive oil

2 tbsp roughly chopped fresh
   flat-leaf parsley

150 ml/5 fl oz crème fraîche

salt and pepper

1 Bring a large pan of lightly salted water to the boil over a medium heat. Add the pasta and cook for about 8–10 minutes, or until tender, but still firm to the bite. Drain well and return to the pan. Add the butter, toss to coat, cover and keep warm.

2 To make the sauce, remove any bones from the tuna and, using 2 forks, flake into smaller pieces. Put the tuna, anchovies, oil and parsley into a food processor and process until smooth. Add the crème fraîche and process for a few seconds to blend. Season to taste with salt and pepper.

3 Shake the pan of pasta over a medium heat for a few minutes, or until it is warmed through.

4 Pour the sauce over the pasta and, using 2 forks, toss quickly. Transfer to 4 large, warmed serving plates and garnish with fresh parsley sprigs. Serve immediately.

pasta & herring salad

serves four

250 g/9 oz dried pasta shells

4 tbsp olive oil

400 g/14 oz rollmop herrings
in brine

6 boiled potatoes

2 large tart apples

2 baby frisée lettuces

2 baby beetroot

4 hard-boiled eggs

6 pickled onions

6 pickled gherkins

2 tbsp capers

3 tbsp tarragon vinegar

salt

1 Bring a large pan of lightly salted water to the boil over a medium heat. Add the pasta and cook for about 8–10 minutes, or until tender, but still firm to the bite. Drain thoroughly, then refresh in cold water.

2 Cut the herrings, potatoes, apples, frisée lettuces and beetroot into small pieces, then put them into a large salad bowl.

3 Drain the pasta thoroughly and add to the salad bowl. Toss lightly with a spoon to mix the pasta and herring mixture together.

4 Carefully shell and slice the eggs and garnish the salad with the egg slices, pickled onions, gherkins and the capers. Sprinkle with the tarragon vinegar and serve immediately.

COOK'S TIP
Store this salad, without the dressing, in a container in the refrigerator.

spaghetti with anchovy & pesto sauce

serves four

6 tablespoons olive oil

2 garlic cloves, crushed

55 g/2 oz canned anchovy
    fillets, drained

450 g/1 lb dried spaghetti

55 g/2 oz Pesto Sauce (see page 20)

2 tbsp finely chopped fresh oregano

85 g/3 oz freshly grated Parmesan
    cheese, plus extra for
    serving (optional)

salt and pepper

4 fresh oregano sprigs, to garnish

COOK'S TIP

If you find canned anchovies too
salty, soak them in a saucer of
cold milk for 5 minutes, drain
and pat dry on kitchen paper
before using.

VARIATION

For a vegetarian alternative of
this recipe, simply substitute
drained sun-dried tomatoes for
the anchovy fillets.

1 Heat the oil in a small pan over a medium heat. Add the crushed garlic and sauté for 3 minutes, then reduce the heat.

2 Stir in the anchovy fillets and cook gently, stirring occasionally with a wooden spoon, until the anchovies have disintegrated.

3 Bring a large pan of lightly salted water to the boil over a medium heat. Add the pasta and cook until just tender, but still firm to the bite.

4 Add the Pesto Sauce (see page 20) and the chopped oregano to the anchovy mixture, then season with pepper to taste.

5 Drain the pasta with a slotted spoon and transfer to 4 warmed serving plates. Pour the Pesto Sauce over the pasta, then sprinkle over the grated Parmesan cheese.

6 Garnish with oregano sprigs and serve with extra cheese (if using).

72

pasta salad with red & white cabbage

serves four

250 g/9 oz dried short-cut macaroni

1 large red cabbage, shredded

1 large white cabbage, shredded

2 large apples, diced

250 g/9 oz cooked smoked bacon
  or ham, diced

4 tbsp olive oil

8 tbsp wine vinegar

1 tbsp sugar

salt and pepper

VARIATION

An alternative dressing for
this salad can be made with
4 tbsp olive oil, 4 tbsp red wine,
4 tbsp red wine vinegar and
1 tbsp sugar.

1 Bring a large pan of lightly salted water to the boil over a medium heat. Add the macaroni and cook until tender, but still firm to the bite. Drain thoroughly, then refresh in cold water. Drain again and reserve.

2 Bring a large pan of lightly salted water to the boil over a medium heat. Add the shredded red cabbage and cook for 5 minutes. Drain thoroughly and leave to cool.

3 Bring a large pan of lightly salted water to the boil over a medium heat. Add the white cabbage and cook for 5 minutes. Drain and leave to cool.

4 Mix the pasta, red cabbage and apple together in a large bowl. Mix the white cabbage and bacon or ham together in a separate bowl.

5 Mix the oil, vinegar and sugar together in another bowl. Season to taste with salt and pepper. Pour the dressing over each of the 2 cabbage mixtures and, finally, mix them all together. Serve immediately.

pasta & chicken medley

serves two

125–150 g/4½–5½ oz dried pasta
    shapes, such as twists or bows

2 tbsp mayonnaise

2 tsp bottled pesto sauce

1 tbsp soured cream or
    fromage frais

175 g/6 oz cooked, skinless,
    boneless chicken meat

1–2 celery sticks

125 g/4½ oz black grapes
    (preferably seedless)

1 large carrot

salt and pepper

celery leaves, to garnish

FRENCH DRESSING

1 tsp wine vinegar

1 tbsp extra virgin olive oil

salt and pepper

1 To make the French dressing, whisk all the ingredients together in a bowl until smooth.

2 Bring a large pan of lightly salted water to the boil over a medium heat. Add the pasta and cook until tender, but still firm to the bite. Drain well, rinse under cold water and drain again. Transfer to a bowl and mix in the French dressing while still hot, then leave until cold.

3 Mix the mayonnaise, pesto sauce and soured cream or fromage frais together in a bowl and season to taste with salt and pepper.

4 Cut the chicken into thin strips. Cut the celery diagonally into thin slices. Reserve a few grapes for garnish, halve the rest and remove any seeds. Cut the carrot into narrow julienne strips.

5 Add the chicken strips, celery, halved grapes, carrot and mayonnaise mixture to the cooled pasta. Toss thoroughly to coat the pasta. Taste and adjust the seasoning, if necessary.

6 Arrange the pasta mixture on 2 serving plates and garnish with the reserved black grapes and the celery leaves. Serve.

niçoise salad with pasta shells

serves four

350 g/12 oz dried pasta shells

115 g/4 oz green beans

50 g/1¾ oz canned anchovy
    fillets, drained

2 tbsp milk

2 small crisp lettuces

450 g/1 lb or 3 large beef tomatoes

4 hard-boiled eggs

225 g/8 oz canned tuna, drained

115 g/4 oz stoned black olives

salt

VINAIGRETTE DRESSING

3 tbsp extra virgin olive oil

2 tbsp white wine vinegar

1 tsp wholegrain mustard

salt and pepper

COOK'S TIP

It is very convenient to make
salad dressings in a screw-top
jar. Put all the ingredients in the
jar, cover securely and shake well
to mix and emulsify the oil.

1 Bring a large pan of lightly salted water to the boil over a medium heat. Add the pasta and cook until tender, but still firm to the bite. Drain and refresh in cold water.

2 Bring a small pan of lightly salted water to the boil over a medium heat. Add the green beans and cook for 10–12 minutes, or until tender but still firm to the bite. Drain, refresh in cold water, drain again and reserve.

3 Put the anchovies in a shallow bowl, pour over the milk and leave to stand for 10 minutes. Meanwhile, tear the lettuces into large pieces. Blanch the tomatoes in boiling water for 1–2 minutes, then drain, skin and roughly chop the flesh. Shell the eggs and cut into quarters. Cut the tuna into large chunks.

4 Drain the anchovies and the pasta. Put the salad ingredients, the green beans and the olives into a large bowl and gently mix together.

5 To make the vinaigrette dressing, beat together all the dressing ingredients and chill in the refrigerator until required. Just before serving, pour the vinaigrette dressing over the salad.

76

rare beef pasta salad

serves four

450 g/1 lb rump or sirloin steak
   in 1 piece
450 g/1 lb dried fusilli
4 tbsp olive oil
2 tbsp lime juice
2 tbsp Thai fish sauce
   (see Cook's Tip)
2 tsp clear honey
4 spring onions, sliced
1 cucumber, peeled and cut into
   2.5-cm/1-inch chunks
3 tomatoes, cut into wedges
3 tsp finely chopped fresh mint
salt and pepper

COOK'S TIP

Thai fish sauce, also known as nam pla, is made from salted anchovies. It has a strong flavour, so should be used with care.

1 Season the steak to taste with salt and pepper, then grill or pan-fry for 4 minutes on each side. Leave to rest for 5 minutes, then, using a sharp knife, slice the steak thinly across the grain and reserve until required.

2 Meanwhile, bring a large pan of lightly salted water to the boil over a medium heat. Add the pasta and cook until tender, but still firm to the bite. Drain thoroughly, refresh in cold water and drain again. Toss the pasta in the oil.

3 Mix the lime juice, fish sauce and honey together in a small pan and cook over a medium heat for about 2 minutes.

4 Add the spring onions, cucumber, chopped tomatoes and mint to the pan, then add the steak and mix well. Season with salt to taste.

5 Transfer the pasta to a large, warmed serving dish and top with the steak and salad mixture. Serve just warm or leave to cool completely.

spicy sausage salad

serves four

125g/4½ oz small dried pasta
    shapes, such as rotelle

2 tbsp olive oil

1 medium onion, chopped

2 garlic cloves, crushed

1 small yellow pepper, deseeded
    and cut into matchsticks

175 g/6 oz spicy pork sausage, such
    as chorizo, Italian pepperoni or
    salami, skinned and sliced

2 tbsp red wine

1 tbsp red wine vinegar

mixed salad leaves, chilled

salt

2 Heat the oil in a pan over a medium heat. Add the onion and fry until translucent. Stir in the garlic, yellow pepper and sliced sausage and cook for about 3–4 minutes, stirring once or twice.

3 Add the wine, wine vinegar and reserved pasta to the pan, stir to blend well and bring the mixture just to the boil over a medium heat.

4 Arrange the chilled salad leaves on to 4 large serving plates, spoon on the warm sausage and pasta mixture and serve immediately.

VARIATION

Other suitable sausages include
the Italian pepperoni, flavoured
with chilli peppers, fennel and
spices and one of the many
varieties of salami, usually
flavoured with garlic and pepper.

1 Bring a pan of lightly salted water to the boil over a medium heat. Add the pasta and and cook until tender. Drain thoroughly and reserve.

goat's cheese, pear & walnut salad

serves four

250 g/9 oz dried penne

1 head radicchio, torn into pieces

1 Webbs lettuce, torn into pieces

7 tbsp chopped walnuts

2 ripe pears, cored and diced

1 bunch watercress, trimmed

2 tbsp lemon juice

5 tbsp olive oil

1 garlic clove, chopped

3 tbsp white wine vinegar

4 tomatoes, quartered

1 small onion, sliced

1 large carrot, grated

250 g/9 oz goat's cheese, diced

salt and pepper

COOK'S TIP

Most goat's cheese comes
from France and there are
many varieties, such as Crottin
de Chavignol, Chabi, which is
very pungent and Sainte-Maure,
which is available in creamery
and farmhouse varieties.

1 Bring a large pan of lightly salted water to the boil over a medium heat. Add the pasta and cook for about 8–10 minutes, or until tender, but still firm to the bite. Drain the pasta, refresh under cold running water, drain again and leave to cool.

2 Put the radicchio and Webbs lettuce into a large salad bowl and mix together well. Top with the pasta, walnuts, pears and watercress.

3 Mix the lemon juice, oil, garlic and vinegar together in a measuring jug. Pour the mixture over the salad ingredients and toss to coat the salad leaves thoroughly.

4 Add the tomato quarters, onion slices, grated carrot and diced goat's cheese and, using 2 forks, toss together until well mixed. Leave the salad to chill in the refrigerator for about 1 hour before serving.

pasta with pesto vinaigrette

serves six

225 g/8 oz dried pasta spirals

4 tomatoes, peeled

55 g/2 oz black olives

25 g/1 oz sun-dried tomatoes in
oil, drained

2 tbsp pine kernels, toasted

2 tbsp Parmesan cheese shavings

1 fresh basil sprig, to garnish

PESTO VINAIGRETTE

4 tbsp chopped fresh basil

1 garlic clove, crushed

2 tbsp freshly grated
Parmesan cheese

4 tbsp olive oil

2 tbsp lemon juice

salt and pepper

1 Bring a large pan of lightly salted water to the boil over a medium heat. Add the pasta and cook for about 8–10 minutes, or until tender, but still firm to the bite. Drain, rinse in hot water, then drain again and reserve.

2 To make the pesto vinaigrette, whisk the basil, garlic, Parmesan cheese, oil and lemon juice together in a small bowl until well blended. Season with pepper to taste.

3 Put the pasta into a bowl, pour the pesto vinaigrette over it and toss thoroughly.

4 Cut the tomatoes into wedges. Halve and stone the olives and slice the sun-dried tomatoes. Add the tomatoes, olives and sun-dried tomatoes to the pasta and toss well.

5 Transfer the pasta mixture to a salad bowl and scatter the pine kernels and Parmesan cheese over the top. Garnish with a fresh basil sprig and serve warm.

dolcelatte, nut & pasta salad

serves four

225 g/8 oz dried pasta shells

1 tbsp olive oil

115 g/4 oz shelled and
   halved walnuts

mixed salad leaves, such as
   radicchio, escarole, rocket,
   lamb's lettuce and frisée

225 g/8 oz dolcelatte
   cheese, crumbled

salt and pepper

DRESSING

2 tbsp walnut oil

4 tbsp extra virgin olive oil

2 tbsp red wine vinegar

3 To make the dressing, whisk the walnut oil, olive oil and vinegar together in a small bowl. Season to taste with salt and pepper.

4 Arrange the mixed salad leaves in a large serving bowl. Pile the cooled pasta in the centre of the salad leaves and sprinkle over the dolcelatte cheese. Pour the dressing over the pasta salad, scatter over the cooled walnut halves and toss together to mix well. Serve immediately.

1 Bring a large pan of lightly salted water to the boil over a medium heat. Add the pasta and cook for about 8–10 minutes, or until just tender, but still firm to the bite. Drain thoroughly, then refresh under cold running water. Drain again and reserve.

2 Spread out the shelled walnut halves on to a large baking tray and toast under a preheated hot grill for 2–3 minutes. Remove and leave to cool while you make the dressing.

avocado, tomato & mozzarella salad

serves four

2 tbsp pine kernels

175 g/6 oz dried fusilli

6 tomatoes

225 g/8 oz mozzarella cheese

1 large avocado pear

2 tbsp lemon juice

3 tbsp chopped fresh basil

salt and pepper

fresh basil sprigs, to garnish

DRESSING

6 tbsp extra virgin olive oil

2 tbsp white wine vinegar

1 tsp wholegrain mustard

pinch of sugar

1 Spread the pine kernels out on to a baking tray and toast under a preheated hot grill for 1–2 minutes. Remove and leave to cool.

2 Bring a large pan of lightly salted water to the boil over a medium heat. Add the pasta and cook until tender, but still firm to the bite. Drain the pasta and refresh in cold water. Drain again and leave to cool.

3 Thinly slice the tomatoes and the mozzarella cheese.

4 Using a sharp knife, cut the avocado pear in half, remove the stone and skin, then cut into thin slices lengthways. Sprinkle with lemon juice to prevent discoloration.

5 To make the dressing, whisk the oil, vinegar, mustard and sugar together in a small bowl. Season to taste with salt and pepper.

6 Arrange the sliced tomatoes, mozzarella cheese and avocado pear alternately in overlapping slices on a large serving platter.

7 Toss the pasta with half the dressing and the chopped basil and season to taste with salt and pepper. Spoon the pasta into the centre of the platter and pour over the remaining dressing. Sprinkle over the pine kernels and garnish with fresh basil sprigs. Serve immediately.

marinated aubergine on a bed of linguine

serves four

150 ml/5 fl oz vegetable stock

150 ml/5 fl oz white wine vinegar

2 tsp balsamic vinegar

3 tbsp olive oil

1 fresh oregano sprig

450 g/1 lb aubergines, peeled and
    sliced thinly

400 g/14 oz dried linguine

MARINADE

2 tbsp extra virgin olive oil

2 garlic cloves, crushed

2 tbsp chopped fresh oregano

2 tbsp finely chopped
    roasted almonds

2 tbsp diced red pepper

2 tbsp lime juice

grated rind and juice of 1 orange

salt and pepper

1 Put the stock, white wine vinegar and balsamic vinegar into a small pan and bring to the boil over a low heat. Add 2 teaspoons of the oil and the oregano sprig and simmer gently for about 1 minute.

2 Add the aubergine slices to the pan, remove from the heat and reserve for 10 minutes.

3 Meanwhile, make the marinade. Mix the oil, garlic, chopped oregano, almonds, red pepper, lime juice, orange rind and juice together in a large bowl. Season to taste with salt and pepper.

4 Carefully remove the aubergine from the pan with a slotted spoon and drain well. Add the aubergine slices to the marinade, mixing well to coat. Cover with clingfilm and chill in the refrigerator for about 12 hours.

5 Bring a large pan of lightly salted water to the boil over a medium heat. Add the pasta and cook for about 8–10 minutes, or until tender, but still firm to the bite.

6 Drain the pasta thoroughly and toss with the remaining oil while it is still warm. Arrange the pasta on a large serving plate with the aubergine slices and the marinade. Serve immediately.

pasta provençale

serves four

225 g/8 oz dried penne

1 tbsp olive oil

25 g/1 oz stoned black olives,
  drained and chopped

25 g/1 oz dry-pack sun-dried
  tomatoes, soaked, drained
  and chopped

400 g/14 oz canned artichoke
  hearts, drained and halved

115 g/4 oz baby courgettes,
  trimmed and sliced

115 g/4 oz baby plum
  tomatoes, halved

100 g/3½ oz assorted salad leaves

salt and pepper

shredded fresh basil leaves,
  to garnish

DRESSING

4 tbsp passata

2 tbsp low-fat natural fromage frais

1 tbsp unsweetened orange juice

1 small bunch fresh basil, shredded

1 Bring a large pan of lightly salted water to the boil over a medium heat. Add the pasta and cook until tender, but still firm to the bite Drain well and return to the pan. Stir in the oil, salt and pepper, olives and sun-dried tomatoes. Leave to cool.

2 Gently mix the artichokes, courgettes and plum tomatoes into the cooked pasta. Arrange the salad leaves in a serving bowl.

VARIATION

For a non-vegetarian version, stir 225 g/8 oz canned tuna in brine, drained and flaked, into the pasta together with the vegetables. Other pasta shapes can be included – look out for farfalle (bows) and rotelle (spoked wheels).

3 To make the dressing, mix all the ingredients together and toss into the vegetables and pasta.

4 Spoon the mixture on top of the salad leaves and garnish with shredded basil leaves. Serve.

Meat & Poultry

Pasta and meat or poultry is a classic combination. Dishes range from easy, economic mid-week suppers to sophisticated and elegant meals for special occasions. The recipes in this chapter include many family favourites, such as Spaghetti Bolognese, Tagliatelle with Meatballs, Lasagne Verde and Cannelloni. There are also some exciting variations on traditional themes, such as Sicilian Spaghetti, Chicken Tortellini and Chicken & Ham Lasagne. Finally, there is a superb collection of mouthwatering original recipes. Why not try Tagliatelle with Pumpkin & Parma Ham, Pasta & Pork in Cream Sauce, Chicken & lobster on Penne or even Breast of Pheasant Lasagne.

pasticcio

250 g/9 oz dried fusilli

4 tbsp double cream

1 tbsp olive oil for brushing

salt and pepper

1 fresh rosemary sprig, to garnish

mixed salad, to serve

SAUCE

2 tbsp olive oil

1 onion, sliced thinly

1 red pepper, deseeded
   and chopped

2 garlic cloves, chopped

600 g/1 lb 5 oz minced beef

400 g/14 oz canned
   chopped tomatoes

125 ml/4 fl oz dry white wine

2 tbsp chopped fresh parsley

55 g/2 oz canned anchovy
   fillets, drained

TOPPING

300 ml/10 fl oz natural yogurt

3 eggs

pinch of freshly grated nutmeg

40 g/1½ oz freshly grated
   Parmesan cheese

1 Make the sauce. Heat the oil in a pan over a medium heat. Add the onion and pepper and fry for 3 minutes. Add the garlic and cook for 1 minute. Add the beef and cook until browned.

2 Add the tomatoes and wine and bring to the boil over a medium heat. Reduce the heat and simmer for about 20 minutes or until thickened. Stir in the parsley and anchovies and season to taste with salt and pepper.

3 Bring a large pan of lightly salted water to the boil over a medium heat. Add the pasta and cook until almost tender. Drain and transfer to a bowl. Stir in the cream.

4 For the topping, beat the yogurt, eggs and nutmeg together.

5 Brush an ovenproof dish with oil. Spoon in half the pasta and cover with half the sauce. Repeat, then spread over the topping and sprinkle with the Parmesan cheese.

6 Bake in a preheated oven at 190°C/375°F/Gas Mark 5, for about 25 minutes, or until golden brown. Garnish with a fresh rosemary sprig and serve with a mixed salad.

lasagne verde

1 tbsp butter for greasing

14 sheets precooked lasagne

850 ml/1½ pints Béchamel Sauce
(see page 98)

85 g/3 oz grated mozzarella cheese

1 fresh basil sprig, to garnish

MEAT SAUCE

2 tbsp olive oil

450 g/1 lb minced beef

1 large onion, chopped

1 celery stick, diced

4 garlic cloves, crushed

25 g/1 oz plain flour

300 ml/10 fl oz beef stock

150 ml/5 fl oz red wine

1 tbsp chopped fresh parsley

1 tsp chopped fresh marjoram

1 tsp chopped fresh basil

2 tbsp tomato purée

salt and pepper

4 Bake the lasagne in a preheated oven at 190°C/375°F/Gas Mark 5, for about 35 minute,s or until the top is golden brown and bubbling. Garnish with a fresh basil sprig and serve immediately.

2 Sprinkle over the flour and cook, stirring, for 1 minute. Gradually stir in the stock and red wine, season with salt and pepper and add the herbs. Bring to the boil and simmer for 35 minutes. Add the tomato purée and simmer for 10 minutes.

3 Lightly grease an ovenproof dish with the butter. Arrange sheets of lasagne over the base, spoon over a layer of meat sauce, then Béchamel Sauce (see page 98). Put another layer of lasagne on top and repeat, finishing with a layer of Béchamel Sauce. Sprinkle over the mozzarella cheese.

1 To make the meat sauce, heat the oil in a large frying pan over a medium heat. Add the minced beef and fry, stirring frequently, until browned all over. Add the onion, celery and garlic and cook for 3 minutes.

tagliatelle with pumpkin & parma ham

serves four

500 g/1 lb 2 oz pumpkin or
    butternut squash, peeled
2 tbsp olive oil
1 onion, chopped finely
2 garlic cloves, crushed
4–6 tbsp chopped fresh parsley
pinch of freshly grated nutmeg
about 250 ml/9 fl oz chicken or
    vegetable stock
115 g/4 oz Parma ham
250 g/9 oz dried tagliatelle
150 ml/5 fl oz double cream
salt and pepper
freshly grated Parmesan cheese,
    to serve

1 Cut the pumpkin or butternut squash in half and scoop out the seeds with a spoon. Cut the pumpkin or squash into 1-cm/½-inch dice.

2 Heat 2 tablespoons of the oil in a large pan over a low heat. Add the onion and garlic and fry for about 3 minutes or until soft. Add half the parsley and fry for 1 minute.

3 Add the pumpkin pieces and cook for 2–3 minutes. Season to taste with salt, pepper and nutmeg.

4 Add half the stock to the pan, bring to the boil over a medium heat, cover and simmer for 10 minutes or until the pumpkin is tender. Add more stock if the pumpkin is becoming dry and looks as if it might burn.

5 Add the Parma ham to the pan and cook, stirring frequently, for a further 2 minutes.

6 Meanwhile, bring a large pan of lightly salted water to the boil over a medium heat. Add the pasta and cook for 12 minutes, or until tender, but still firm to the bite. Drain the pasta thoroughly and transfer to a large, warmed serving dish.

7 Stir the cream into the pumpkin and ham mixture and heat through. Spoon over the pasta, sprinkle over the remaining parsley and serve. Serve the Parmesan cheese separately.

stuffed cannelloni

8 dried cannelloni tubes

25 g/1 oz freshly grated
   Parmesan cheese

fresh herb sprigs, to garnish

FILLING

2 tbsp butter

300 g/10½ oz frozen spinach,
   thawed, drained and chopped

115 g/4 oz ricotta cheese

25 g/1 oz freshly grated
   Parmesan cheese

55 g/2 oz chopped ham

pinch of freshly grated nutmeg

2 tbsp double cream

2 eggs, lightly beaten

salt and pepper

BECHAMEL SAUCE

2 tbsp butter

2½ tbsp plain flour

300 ml/10 fl oz milk

2 bay leaves

pinch of freshly grated nutmeg

1 To make the filling, melt the
   butter in a pan over a low heat.
Add the spinach and fry for 2–3 minutes.
Remove from the heat and stir in the
ricotta and Parmesan cheeses and the
ham. Season to taste with nutmeg, salt
and pepper. Beat in the cream and
eggs to make a thick paste.

2 Bring a large pan of lightly salted
   water to the boil over a medium
heat. Add the cannelloni tubes and
cook for 10–12 minutes, or until
almost tender. Drain and leave to cool.

3 To make the sauce, melt the
   butter in a pan over a low heat.
Stir in the flour and cook, stirring, for
1 minute. Gradually whisk in the milk.
Add the bay leaves and simmer,
whisking, for 5 minutes. Add the
nutmeg, salt and pepper. Remove from
the heat and discard the bay leaves.

4 Spoon the filling into a piping bag
   and use to fill the cannelloni.

5 Spoon a little sauce into the base
   of an ovenproof dish and place
the cannelloni in a single layer on the
sauce. Pour over the remaining sauce.
Sprinkle the Parmesan cheese over the
top and bake in a preheated oven at
190°C/375°F/Gas Mark 5, for about
40–45 minutes. Garnish with fresh
herb sprigs and serve immediately.

sicilian spaghetti

serves four

150 ml/5 fl oz olive oil, plus extra
  for brushing

2 aubergines

350 g/12 oz minced beef

1 onion, chopped

2 garlic cloves, crushed

2 tbsp tomato purée

400 g/14 oz canned
  chopped tomatoes

1 tsp Worcestershire sauce

1 tsp chopped fresh marjoram or
  oregano or ½ tsp dried marjoram
  or oregano

55 g/2 oz stoned black olives, sliced

1 green, red or yellow pepper,
  deseeded and chopped

175 g/6 oz dried spaghetti

115 g/4 oz freshly grated
  Parmesan cheese

salt and pepper

1 Brush a 20-cm/8-inch loose-based
round cake tin with oil, then line
the base with non-stick baking paper
and brush with a little oil.

2 Slice the aubergines. Heat a little
oil in a pan over a low heat. Add
the aubergines, in batches and fry until
browned on both sides. Add more oil,
as necessary. Drain on kitchen paper.

3 Put the beef, onion and garlic into
a pan and cook over a medium
heat until browned. Add the tomato
purée, tomatoes, Worcestershire sauce,
marjoram and salt and pepper. Simmer
for 10 minutes. Add the olives and
pepper and cook for 10 minutes.

4 Bring a pan of lightly salted water
to the boil over a medium heat.
Add the pasta and cook until tender,
but still firm to the bite. Drain the pasta
thoroughly and transfer to a bowl. Add
the meat mixture and Parmesan cheese
and toss with 2 forks.

5 Arrange aubergine slices over the
base and up the sides of the tin.
Add the pasta, then cover with the rest
of the aubergines. Bake in a preheated
oven at 200°C/400°F/Gas Mark 6,
for 40 minutes. Leave to stand for
5 minutes, then invert on to a serving
dish. Discard the paper and serve.

cannelloni

serves four

225 g/8 oz lean minced beef

1 large red onion, chopped finely

150 g/5½ oz button
   mushrooms, chopped

1 garlic clove, crushed

½ tsp ground nutmeg

1 tsp dried mixed herbs

2 tbsp tomato purée

4 tbsp dry red wine

12 dried 'quick cook' cannelloni tubes

salt and pepper

mixed salad, to serve

TOMATO SAUCE

1 red onion, chopped finely

1 large carrot, grated

1 celery stick, chopped finely

1 bay leaf

150 ml/5 fl oz dry red wine

400 g/14 oz canned
   chopped tomatoes

2 tbsp tomato purée

1 tsp caster sugar

salt and pepper

TO GARNISH

25 g/1 oz fresh Parmesan
   cheese shavings

1 plum tomato

1 fresh basil sprig

1 Put the beef, onion, mushrooms and garlic into a non-stick pan and fry over a low heat for 3–4 minutes. Stir in the nutmeg, herbs, seasoning, tomato purée and wine. Simmer for 15–20 minutes. Cool for 10 minutes.

2 To make the sauce, put the onion, carrot, celery, bay leaf and wine into a pan. Bring to the boil and simmer for 5 minutes. Add the other sauce ingredients and cook for about 15 minutes. Discard the bay leaf.

3 Spoon a quarter of the sauce into the base of an ovenproof dish. Fill the cannelloni with the meat mixture and arrange on the sauce. Spoon over remaining sauce. Bake in a preheated oven at 200°C/400°F/Gas Mark 6, for 35–40 minutes. Garnish with the cheese, tomato and basil sprig. Serve.

spaghetti bolognese

serves four

1 tbsp olive oil

1 onion, chopped finely

2 garlic cloves, chopped

1 carrot, chopped

1 celery stick, chopped

50 g/1¾ oz pancetta or streaky
  bacon, diced

350 g/12 oz lean minced beef

400 g/14 oz canned
  chopped tomatoes

2 tsp dried oregano

125 ml/4 fl oz red wine

2 tbsp tomato purée

675 g/1½ lb fresh spaghetti or
  350 g/12 oz dried spaghetti

salt and pepper

VARIATION

Try adding 25 g/1 oz dried
porcini, soaked for 20 minutes in
2 tbsp of warm water,
to the bolognese sauce in
step 4, if you wish.

1 Heat the oil in a large frying pan over a low heat. Add the onion and cook for 3 minutes.

2 Add the garlic, carrot, celery and pancetta or bacon to the pan and sauté for 3–4 minutes, or until just starting to brown.

3 Add the beef and cook over a high heat for another 3 minutes, or until the meat has browned.

4 Stir in the tomatoes, oregano and red wine and bring to the boil. Reduce the heat and simmer for about 45 minutes.

5 Stir in the tomato purée and season with salt and pepper.

6 Bring a large pan of lightly salted water to the boil over a medium heat. Add the pasta and cook for about 8–10 minutes, or until tender, but still firm to the bite. Drain thoroughly.

7 Transfer the pasta to 4 serving plates and pour over the sauce. Toss to mix well and serve.

red spiced beef

serves four

625 g/1 lb 6 oz sirloin or rump steak

2 tbsp paprika

2–3 tsp mild chilli powder

½ tsp salt

6 celery sticks

6 tbsp stock or water

2 tbsp tomato purée

2 tbsp clear honey

1 tbsp Worcestershire sauce

3 tbsp wine vinegar

2 tbsp sunflower oil

4 spring onions, thinly
    sliced diagonally

4 tomatoes, peeled, deseeded
    and sliced

1–2 garlic cloves, crushed

celery leaves, to garnish (optional)

cooked Chinese noodles, to serve

1 Cut the steak across the grain into narrow strips, about 1-cm/ ½-inch thick and put into a bowl.

2 Mix the paprika, chilli powder and salt together. Add to the beef and mix until the beef is evenly coated with the spices. Leave to marinate in the refrigerator for at least 30 minutes.

3 Cut the celery into 5-cm/2-inch lengths, then cut the lengths into strips about 5-mm/¼-inch thick.

4 Mix the stock, tomato purée, honey, Worcestershire sauce and vinegar together and reserve.

5 Heat a wok over a high heat. Add the oil and when hot, add the spring onions, celery, tomatoes and garlic. Stir-fry for 1 minute, then add the steak. Stir-fry for 3–4 minutes until the meat is sealed. Add the sauce and stir-fry until coated and sizzling.

6 Garnish with celery leaves (if using) and serve with noodles.

spiced fried minced pork

serves four

2 tbsp sunflower oil

2 garlic cloves, chopped finely

3 shallots, chopped finely

2 tsp finely chopped fresh
    root ginger

500 g/1 lb 2 oz lean minced pork

2 tbsp Thai fish sauce

1 tbsp dark soy sauce

1 tbsp red curry paste

4 dried kaffir lime leaves, crumbled

4 plum tomatoes, chopped

3 tbsp chopped fresh coriander

salt and pepper

fresh coriander leaves, to garnish

boiled fine egg noodles, to serve

1 Heat a wok over a medium heat. Add the oil and, when hot, add the garlic, shallots and ginger. Stir-fry for about 2 minutes. Stir in the pork and stir-fry until golden brown.

2 Stir in the fish sauce, soy sauce, red curry paste and lime leaves and stir-fry for a further 1–2 minutes over a high heat.

3 Add the chopped tomatoes and cook, stirring occasionally, for a further 5–6 minutes.

4 Stir in the chopped coriander and season to taste with salt and pepper. Pile boiled fine egg noodles on to 4 large, warmed serving plates and spoon on the spiced pork. Garnish with a few fresh coriander leaves and serve immediately.

tagliatelle with meatballs

serves four

500 g/1 lb 2 oz lean minced beef

55 g/2 oz soft white breadcrumbs

1 garlic clove, crushed

2 tbsp chopped fresh parsley

1 tsp dried oregano

pinch of freshly grated nutmeg

¼ tsp ground coriander

55 g/2 oz freshly grated Parmesan
cheese, plus extra, to serve

2–3 tbsp milk

plain flour, for dusting

3 tbsp olive oil

400 g/14 oz dried tagliatelle

2 tbsp butter, diced

salt and pepper

mixed salad, to serve

TOMATO SAUCE

3 tbsp olive oil

2 large onions, sliced

2 celery sticks, sliced thinly

2 garlic cloves, chopped

400 g/14 oz canned
chopped tomatoes

125 g/4½ oz sun-dried tomatoes in
oil, drained and chopped

2 tbsp tomato purée

1 tbsp dark muscovado sugar

150 ml/5 fl oz white wine or water

1 To make the sauce, heat the oil in a frying pan over a high heat. Add the onions and celery and cook until translucent. Add the garlic and cook for 1 minute. Stir in the tomatoes, tomato purée, sugar and wine. Season with salt and pepper. Bring to the boil and simmer for 10 minutes.

2 Meanwhile, break up the beef in a large bowl until it becomes a sticky paste. Stir in the breadcrumbs, garlic, herbs and spices. Stir in the Parmesan cheese and enough milk to make a firm paste. Lightly flour your hands, take large spoonfuls of the mixture and shape it into 12 balls. Heat the oil in a large frying pan over a medium heat. Add the meatballs and fry for 5–6 minutes or until browned.

3 Pour the tomato sauce over the meatballs. Reduce the heat, cover the pan and simmer for 30 minutes, turning once or twice. Add a little extra water if the sauce is starting to become too dry.

4 Bring a large pan of lightly salted water to the boil over a medium heat. Add the pasta and cook for 8–10 minutes, or until tender, but still firm to the bite. Drain, then transfer to a serving dish, dot with the butter and toss with 2 forks. Spoon the meatballs and sauce over the pasta, then transfer to 4 serving plates and serve with Parmesan cheese and a mixed salad.

neopolitan veal cutlets with mascarpone

serves four

200 g/7 oz butter

4 x 250 g/9 oz veal cutlets, trimmed

1 large onion, sliced

2 apples, peeled, cored and sliced

175 g/6 oz button mushrooms

1 tbsp chopped fresh tarragon

8 black peppercorns

1 tbsp sesame seeds

400 g/14 oz dried marille

100 ml/3½ fl oz extra virgin olive oil

175 g/6 oz mascarpone cheese,
    broken into small pieces

2 large beef tomatoes, cut in half

leaves of 1 fresh basil sprig

salt and pepper

1 Melt 55 g/2 oz of the butter in a pan over a low heat. Add the veal and fry for 5 minutes on each side. Transfer to a dish and keep warm.

2 Fry the onion and apples in the pan until lightly browned. Transfer to a dish, put the veal on top and keep warm.

3 Melt the remaining butter in the pan over a low heat. Add the mushrooms, tarragon and peppercorns and gently fry for 3 minutes. Sprinkle over the sesame seeds.

4 Bring a large pan of lightly salted water to the boil over a medium heat. Add the pasta and cook until tender, but still firm to the bite. Drain and transfer to an large ovenproof serving dish.

5 Top the pasta with the mascarpone cheese and sprinkle over the remaining oil. Put the onions, apples and veal cutlets on top. Spoon the mushrooms and peppercorns on to the cutlets, arrange the tomatoes and basil leaves around the edge and season to taste with salt and pepper. Cook in a preheated oven at 150°C/300°F/Gas Mark 2, for about 5 minutes.

6 Remove from the oven and transfer to 4 plates, then serve.

fettuccine with veal in a rose petal sauce

serves four

450 g/1 lb dried fettuccine

6 tbsp olive oil

1 tsp chopped fresh oregano

1 tsp chopped fresh marjoram

175 g/6 oz butter

450 g/1 lb veal fillet, sliced thinly

150 ml/5 fl oz rose petal vinegar
   (see Cook's Tip)

150 ml/5 fl oz fish stock

3 tbsp grapefruit juice

3 tbsp double cream

salt

TO GARNISH

12 pink grapefruit segments

12 pink peppercorns

rose petals, washed

COOK'S TIP

To make rose petal vinegar, infuse the rinsed petals of 8 pesticide-free roses in 150 ml/5 fl oz white wine vinegar for 48 hours.

1 Bring a large pan of lightly salted water to the boil over a medium heat. Add the pasta and cook for about 12 minutes, or until tender, but still firm to the bite. Drain the pasta and transfer to a warmed serving dish, sprinkle over 2 tablespoons of the oil, the oregano and marjoram.

2 Heat 55 g/2 oz of the butter with the remaining oil in a large frying pan over a low heat. Add the veal and cook for 6 minutes. Remove the veal from the pan and put on top of the pasta. Keep warm.

3 Add the vinegar and stock to the pan and bring to the boil over a medium heat. Boil vigorously until reduced by two thirds. Reduce the heat, add the grapefruit juice and cream and simmer over a low heat for 4 minutes. Dice the remaining butter and add to the pan, a piece at a time,

whisking constantly, until it has been completely incorporated.

4 Pour the sauce around the veal, garnish with grapefruit segments, pink peppercorns and rose petals. Serve immediately.

creamed strips of sirloin with rigatoni

serves four

85 g/3 oz butter

450 g/1 lb sirloin steak, trimmed
and cut into thin strips

175 g/6 oz button
mushrooms, sliced

1 tsp mustard

pinch of freshly grated root ginger

2 tbsp dry sherry

150 ml/5 fl oz double cream

450 g/1 lb dried rigatoni

2 fresh basil sprigs

115 g/4 oz butter

salt and pepper

4 slices hot toast, cut into triangles,
to serve

COOK'S TIP

Dried pasta will keep for up to
6 months. Keep it in the packet
and reseal it once you have
opened it, or transfer the pasta
to an airtight jar.

1 Melt the butter in a large frying
pan over a low heat. Add the
steak, and fry gently, stirring frequently,
for 6 minutes. Transfer the steak to a
large ovenproof dish with a slotted
spoon and keep warm.

2 Add the sliced mushrooms to
the frying pan and cook for
2–3 minutes in the juices remaining in
the pan. Add the mustard, grated
ginger, salt and pepper. Cook for about
2 minutes, then add the sherry and
cream. Cook for a further 3 minutes,
then pour the sauce over the steak.

3 Bake the steak in a preheated
oven at 190°C/375°F/ Gas
Mark 5, for 10 minutes.

4 Meanwhile, bring a large pan of
lightly salted water to the boil
over a medium heat. Add the pasta
and 1 of the basil sprigs and cook for
10 minutes, or until tender, but still
firm to the bite. Drain the pasta and
transfer to a warmed serving plate.
Toss the pasta with the butter and
garnish with the other basil sprig.

5 Transfer the steak to 4 warmed
serving plates and serve with the
pasta and triangles of hot toast.

drunken noodles

serves four

175 g/6 oz rice stick noodles

2 tbsp vegetable oil

1 garlic clove, crushed

2 small fresh green chillies, chopped

1 small onion, sliced thinly

150 g/5½ oz lean minced pork
    or chicken

1 small green pepper, deseeded and
    chopped finely

4 kaffir lime leaves, shredded finely

1 tbsp dark soy sauce

1 tbsp light soy sauce

½ tsp sugar

1 tomato, cut into thin wedges

2 tbsp fresh sweet basil leaves,
    shredded finely, to garnish

COOK'S TIP

Fresh kaffir lime leaves freeze
well, so if you buy more than
you need, simply tie them in a
tightly sealed plastic freezer bag
and freeze for up to a month.
They can be used straight
from the freezer.

1 Put the noodles into a bowl and pour over enough hot water to cover. Soak for 15 minutes or according to the packet instructions. Drain well.

2 Heat a large wok over a high heat. Add the oil and when hot, add the garlic, chillies and onion and stir-fry for 1 minute.

3 Stir in the meat and stir-fry over a high heat for 1 minute, then add the pepper and stir-fry for 2 minutes.

4 Stir in the lime leaves, soy sauces and sugar. Add the noodles and tomato and toss to heat thoroughly.

5 Transfer to 4 large, warmed serving plates and sprinkle with the shredded basil. Serve immediately.

venison meatballs with kumquat sauce

serves four

450 g/1 lb lean minced venison

1 small leek, chopped finely

1 medium carrot, grated finely

½ tsp ground nutmeg

1 medium egg white, beaten lightly

salt and pepper

KUMQUAT SAUCE

100 g/3½ oz kumquats

1 tbsp caster sugar

150 ml/5 fl oz water

4 tbsp dry sherry

1 tsp cornflour

TO SERVE

freshly cooked pasta or noodles

freshly cooked vegetables

1 Put the venison into a bowl together with the leek, carrot, seasoning and nutmeg. Add the egg white and bind the ingredients together with your hands until the mixture is well moulded and firm.

2 Divide the mixture into 16 equal portions. Form each portion into a small round ball with your fingers.

3 Bring a large pan of water to the boil over a medium heat. Arrange the meatballs on a layer of baking paper in a steamer and put over the boiling water. Cover and steam for 10 minutes, or until cooked through.

4 To make the sauce, wash and slice the kumquats thinly, then put into a pan with the sugar and water. Bring to the boil over a low heat and cook for 2–3 minutes until tender.

5 Blend the sherry and cornflour together and add to the pan. Heat, stirring, until the sauce thickens. Season to taste with salt and pepper.

6 Drain the meatballs and transfer to a serving plate. Spoon over the sauce and serve with freshly cooked pasta and vegetables.

pasta & pork in cream sauce

serves four

450 g/1 lb pork fillet, sliced thinly

4 tbsp olive oil

225 g/8 oz button
   mushrooms, sliced

200 ml/7 fl oz Italian Red Wine
   Sauce (see page 96)

1 tbsp lemon juice

pinch of saffron

350 g/12 oz dried orecchioni

4 tbsp double cream

12 quail eggs (see Cook's Tip)

salt

COOK'S TIP

In this recipe, the quail eggs are
soft-boiled. As they are
extremely difficult to shell when
warm, it is important that they
are thoroughly cooled first.
Otherwise, they will break up
unattractively.

1 Put the pork slices between
2 sheets of clingfilm and pound
until wafer thin, then cut into strips.

2 Heat the oil in a large frying pan
over a medium heat. Add the
pork strips and stir-fry for 5 minutes.
Add the mushrooms to the pan and
stir-fry for a further 2 minutes.

3 Pour over the Italian Red Wine
Sauce (see page 96), reduce the
heat and simmer gently for 20 minutes.

4 Meanwhile, bring a large pan of
lightly salted water to the boil
over a medium heat. Add the lemon
juice, saffron and pasta and cook for
8–10 minutes, or until tender, but still
firm to the bite. Drain and keep warm.

5 Stir the cream into the pan with
the pork and heat gently for a
few minutes.

6 Boil the eggs for 3 minutes in a
small pan of boiling water. Cool
in cold water and remove the shells.

7 Transfer the pasta to a large,
warmed serving plate, top with
the pork and the sauce and garnish
with the eggs. Serve immediately.

grilled chicken with lemon & honey

serves four

4 boneless chicken breasts (about
   125 g/4¼ oz each)

2 tbsp clear honey

1 tbsp dark soy sauce

1 tsp finely grated lemon rind

1 tbsp lemon juice

salt and pepper

lemon rind strips, to garnish

NOODLES

225 g/8 oz rice noodles

2 tsp sesame oil

1 tbsp sesame seeds

1 tsp finely grated lemon rind

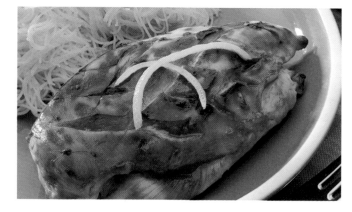

1 Using a sharp knife, skin and trim the chicken breasts to remove any excess fat, then wash and pat dry on kitchen paper. Score the chicken breasts with a criss-cross pattern on both sides (making sure that you do not cut all the way through the meat).

2 Mix the honey, soy sauce, lemon rind and juice together in a small bowl, then season well with pepper.

3 Arrange the chicken breasts on the grill rack so they do not overlap and brush with half the honey mixture. Cook under a preheated medium-hot grill for 10 minutes, turn over and brush with the remaining mixture. Cook for 8–10 minutes, or until cooked through.

4 Meanwhile, prepare the noodles according to the instructions on the packet. Drain well and pile into a warmed serving bowl. Mix the noodles with the sesame oil, sesame seeds and lemon rind. Season and keep warm.

5 Drain the chicken and transfer to 4 warmed serving plates with a small mound of noodles. Garnish with lemon rind strips. Serve immediately.

rice noodles with chicken

serves four

200 g/7 oz rice stick noodles

1 tbsp sunflower oil

1 garlic clove, chopped finely

2-cm/¾-inch piece fresh root ginger,
    chopped finely

4 spring onions, chopped

1 fresh red bird-eye chilli, deseeded
    and sliced

300 g/10½ oz skinless, boneless
    chicken, chopped finely

2 chicken livers, chopped finely

1 celery stick, sliced thinly

1 carrot, cut into fine batons

300 g/10½ oz shredded
    Chinese leaves

4 tbsp lime juice

2 tbsp Thai fish sauce

1 tbsp soy sauce

2 tbsp shredded fresh mint

pickled garlic slices

1 fresh mint sprig, to garnish

1 Put the noodles into a bowl and pour over enough hot water to cover. Soak for 15 minutes or according to the packet instructions. Drain well.

2 Heat the oil in a large frying pan over a high heat. Add the garlic, ginger, spring onions and chilli and stir-fry for 1 minute. Stir in the chicken and chicken livers, then stir-fry for 2–3 minutes, until starting to brown.

3 Stir in the celery and carrot and stir-fry for 2 minutes to soften. Add the Chinese leaves, then stir in the lime juice, fish sauce and soy sauce.

4 Add the noodles and stir to heat through. Sprinkle with the shredded mint and pickled garlic slices. Garnish with a mint sprig and serve.

egg noodles with beef & pasta

serves four

275 g/9½ oz egg noodles

3 tbsp walnut oil

2.5-cm/1-inch piece fresh root
  ginger, cut into thin strips

5 spring onions, shredded finely

2 garlic cloves, chopped finely

1 red pepper, deseeded and
  sliced thinly

100 g/3½ oz button mushrooms,
  sliced thinly

350 g/12 oz fillet steak, cut into
  thin strips

1 tbsp cornflour

5 tbsp dry sherry

3 tbsp soy sauce

1 tsp soft brown sugar

225 g/8 oz bean sprouts

1 tbsp sesame oil

salt and pepper

spring onion strips, to garnish

1 Bring a large pan of water to the boil over a medium heat. Add the noodles and cook according to the

packet instructions. Drain the noodles well and reserve.

2 Heat a wok over a high heat. Add the walnut oil and when hot, add the ginger, spring onions and garlic. Stir-fry for 45 seconds. Add the pepper, mushrooms and steak and stir-fry for about 4 minutes. Season to taste with salt and pepper.

3 Mix the cornflour, sherry and soy sauce together in a small jug to form a smooth paste, then pour into the wok. Sprinkle over the brown sugar and stir-fry all of the ingredients for a further 2 minutes.

4 Add the bean sprouts, noodles and sesame oil to the wok, stir and toss together for 1 minute. Transfer to 4 large serving bowls and garnish with spring onion strips. Serve.

COOK'S TIP

If you do not have a wok, you could prepare this dish in a frying pan. However, a wok is preferable, as the round base ensures an even distribution of heat and it is easier to keep stirring and tossing the contents when stir-frying.

lemon chicken conchiglie

serves four

8 chicken pieces (about
115 g/4 oz each)
55 g/2 oz butter, melted
4 tbsp mild mustard (see Cook's Tip)
2 tbsp lemon juice
1 tbsp brown sugar
1 tsp paprika
3 tbsp poppy seeds
400 g/14 oz fresh pasta shells
salt and pepper

COOK'S TIP

Dijon is the type of mustard most
often used in cooking, as it has a
clean and only mildly spicy
flavour. German mustard has a
sweet-sour taste, with Bavarian
mustard being slightly sweeter.
American mustard is mild
and sweet.

1 Arrange the chicken pieces, smooth-side down, in a single layer in a large ovenproof dish.

2 Mix the butter, mustard, lemon juice, sugar and paprika together in a bowl and season to taste with salt and pepper. Brush the mixture over the upper surfaces of the chicken pieces and bake in a preheated oven at 200°C/400°F/Gas Mark 6, for 15 minutes.

3 Remove the dish from the oven and, using tongs, carefully turn over the chicken pieces. Coat the upper surfaces of the chicken with the remaining mustard mixture and sprinkle with poppy seeds. Return to the oven for a further 15 minutes.

4 Meanwhile, bring a large pan of lightly salted water to the boil over a medium heat. Add the pasta shells and cook until tender, but still firm to the bite.

5 Drain the pasta and arrange in a warmed serving dish. Top with the chicken, then pour over the sauce and serve immediately.

chicken suprêmes filled with tiger prawns

serves four

4 x 200 g/7 oz chicken
   suprêmes, trimmed
115 g/4 oz large spinach leaves,
   trimmed and blanched in hot
   salted water
4 slices of Parma ham
12–16 raw tiger prawns, peeled
   and deveined
450 g/1 lb dried tagliatelle
55 g/2 oz butter, plus extra
   for greasing
3 leeks, shredded
1 large carrot, grated
150 ml/5 fl oz thick mayonnaise
2 large, cooked beetroot
salt

1 Grease 4 large pieces of tinfoil
and reserve. Put each suprême
between 2 pieces of baking paper and
pound with a rolling pin to flatten.

2 Divide half the spinach and put
on top of the suprêmes, add a
slice of ham to each and top with more
spinach, then put 3–4 prawns on top.
Fold the pointed end of the suprême
over the prawns, then fold over again
to form a parcel. Wrap in the tinfoil,
put on to a baking tray and bake in a
preheated oven at 200°C/400°F/
Gas Mark 6, for 20 minutes.

3 Meanwhile, bring a pan of lightly
salted water to the boil over a
medium heat. Add the pasta and cook
until tender, but still firm to the bite.
Drain and transfer to a serving dish.

4 Melt the butter in a frying pan
over a low heat. Add the leeks
and carrot and fry for 3 minutes, then
transfer the vegetables to the centre of
the pasta.

5 Put the mayonnaise and 1 of the
beetroots in a food processor or
blender and process until smooth. Rub
through a sieve and pour around the
pasta and vegetables.

6 Cut the remaining beetroot into
diamond shapes and put neatly
around the mayonnaise. Remove the
tinfoil from the chicken and cut the
suprêmes into thin slices with a sharp
knife. Arrange the slices on top of the
pasta and vegetables, then serve.

chicken & ham lasagne

serves four

1 tbsp butter for greasing

14 sheets precooked lasagne

300 ml/10 fl oz Béchamel Sauce
   (see page 98)

85 g/3 oz freshly grated
   Parmesan cheese

CHICKEN & WILD
MUSHROOM SAUCE

2 tbsp olive oil

2 garlic cloves, crushed

1 large onion, chopped finely

225 g/8 oz wild mushrooms, sliced

300 g/10½ oz minced chicken

85 g/3 oz chicken livers,
   chopped finely

115 g/4 oz Parma ham, diced

150 ml/5 fl oz Marsala wine

280 g/10 oz canned
   chopped tomatoes

1 tbsp chopped fresh basil leaves

2 tbsp tomato purée

salt and pepper

1 To make the chicken and wild mushroom sauce, heat the oil in a large pan over a low heat. Add the garlic, onion and mushrooms and cook, stirring frequently, for 6 minutes.

2 Add the minced chicken, chicken livers and Parma ham and cook, stirring frequently, for 12 minutes, or until the meat has browned.

3 Stir in the Marsala, tomatoes, basil and tomato purée and cook for 4 minutes. Season to taste with salt and pepper, cover and simmer for about 30 minutes. Uncover, stir and simmer for a further 15 minutes.

4 Grease an ovenproof dish with butter. Arrange sheets of lasagne over the base, spoon over a layer of the chicken and mushroom sauce, then spoon over a layer of Béchamel Sauce (see page 98). Put another layer of lasagne on top and repeat the process twice, finishing with a layer of Béchamel Sauce. Sprinkle over the cheese and bake in a preheated oven at 190°C/375°F/Gas Mark 5, for about 35 minutes, or until golden and bubbling. Serve immediately.

chicken & spinach lasagne

serves four

350 g/12 oz frozen chopped
spinach, thawed and drained

½ tsp ground nutmeg

450 g/1 lb lean, cooked chicken
meat, skinned and diced

4 sheets precooked lasagne verde

1½ tbsp cornflour

425 ml/15 fl oz skimmed milk

70 g/2½ oz freshly grated
Parmesan cheese

salt and pepper

TOMATO SAUCE

400 g/14 oz canned
chopped tomatoes

1 onion, chopped finely

1 garlic clove, crushed

150 ml/5 fl oz white wine

3 tbsp tomato purée

1 tsp dried oregano

2 Drain the spinach again and spread it out on kitchen paper to make sure that as much water as possible is removed. Layer the spinach in the base of a large ovenproof baking dish. Sprinkle with ground nutmeg and season to taste with salt and pepper.

3 Arrange the diced chicken over the spinach and spoon over the tomato sauce. Arrange the sheets of lasagne over the tomato sauce.

4 Blend the cornflour with a little of the milk to make a paste. Pour the remaining milk into a pan and stir in the paste. Heat, stirring, until the sauce thickens. Season well.

5 Spoon the sauce over the lasagne and transfer the dish to a baking tray. Sprinkle the grated cheese over the sauce and bake in a preheated oven at 190°C/375°F/Gas Mark 5, for 25 minutes until golden, then serve.

1 To make the tomato sauce, put the tomatoes into a pan and stir in the onion, garlic, wine, tomato purée and oregano. Bring to the boil and simmer for 20 minutes until thick. Season well with salt and pepper.

pasta with chicken sauce

serves four

250 g/9 oz fresh green tagliatelle

1 tbsp olive oil

salt and pepper

fresh basil leaves, to garnish

TOMATO SAUCE

2 tbsp olive oil

1 small onion, chopped

1 garlic clove, chopped

400 g/14 oz canned

   chopped tomatoes

2 tbsp chopped fresh parsley

1 tsp dried oregano

2 bay leaves

2 tbsp tomato purée

1 tsp sugar

CHICKEN SAUCE

55 g/2 oz unsalted butter

400 g/14 oz boned chicken breasts,

   skinned and cut into thin strips

85 g/3 oz blanched almonds

300 ml/10 fl oz double cream

1 To make the tomato sauce, heat the oil in a pan over a medium heat. Add the onion and fry until translucent. Add the garlic and fry for 1 minute. Stir in the tomatoes, parsley, oregano, bay leaves, tomato purée and sugar. Season to taste with salt and pepper, bring to the boil and simmer, uncovered, for 15–20 minutes, until reduced by half. Remove the pan from the heat and discard the bay leaves.

2 To make the chicken sauce, melt the butter in a frying pan over a medium heat. Add the chicken and almonds and stir-fry for 5–6 minutes, or until the chicken is cooked through.

3 Meanwhile, bring the cream to the boil in a small pan over a low heat and boil for about 10 minutes, until reduced by almost half. Pour the cream over the chicken and almonds, stir and season to taste with salt and pepper. Reserve and keep warm.

4 Bring a large pan of lightly salted water to the boil over a medium heat. Add the pasta and cook for about 8–10 minutes, or until tender, but still firm to the bite. Drain and transfer to a warmed serving dish. Spoon over the tomato sauce and arrange the chicken sauce down the centre. Garnish with fresh basil leaves and serve.

chicken & lobster on penne

1 tbsp butter for greasing

6 chicken suprêmes

450 g/1 lb dried penne

2–3 tbsp extra virgin olive oil

85 g/3 oz freshly grated
   Parmesan cheese

salt and pepper

fresh parsley leaves, to garnish

FILLING

115 g/4 oz lobster meat, chopped

2 shallots, very finely chopped

2 figs, chopped

1 tbsp Marsala wine

25 g/1 oz fresh breadcrumbs

1 large egg, beaten

1 Grease 6 pieces of tinfoil large enough to enclose each chicken suprême and grease a baking tray.

2 Put all of the filling ingredients into a mixing bowl and blend together thoroughly with a spoon.

3 Using a sharp knife, cut a pocket in each chicken suprême and fill with the lobster mixture. Wrap each chicken suprême in a piece of tinfoil, put the parcels on to the greased baking tray. Bake in a preheated oven at 200°C/ 400°F/Gas Mark 6, for about 30 minutes.

4 Meanwhile, bring a large pan of lightly salted water to the boil over a medium heat. Add the pasta and cook for 8–10 minutes, or until tender, but still firm to the bite. Drain thoroughly and transfer to a large serving plate. Sprinkle over the remaining oil and the Parmesan cheese. Reserve and keep warm.

5 Carefully remove the tinfoil from around the chicken suprêmes. Using a sharp knife, slice the suprêmes very thinly and arrange over the pasta. Garnish with plenty of fresh parsley and serve immediately.

2

3

3

chicken tortellini

serves four

115 g/4 oz boned chicken
   breast, skinned

55 g/2 oz Parma ham

40 g/1½ oz cooked spinach,
   well drained

1 tbsp finely chopped onion

2 tbsp freshly grated Parmesan cheese

pinch of ground allspice

1 egg, beaten

450 g/1 lb Homemade Pasta Dough
   (see page 50)

plain flour for dusting

salt and pepper

2 tbsp chopped fresh parsley,
   to garnish

SAUCE

300 ml/10 fl oz single cream

2 garlic cloves, crushed

115 g/4 oz button mushrooms,
   sliced thinly

4 tbsp freshly grated
   Parmesan cheese

1 Bring a pan of salted water to the boil over a medium heat. Add the chicken and poach for 10 minutes. Cool, then put into a food processor, with the Parma ham, spinach and onion and process until chopped finely. Stir in 2 tablespoons of the Parmesan cheese, allspice and beaten egg and season to taste with salt and pepper.

2 Put the pasta dough on a floured work surface and roll out thinly. Cut into 4–5-cm/1½–2-inch rounds.

3 Put ½ teaspoon of the filling into the centre of each round. Fold the

pieces in half and press the edges to seal. Wrap each piece around your index finger, cross over the ends and curl the rest of the dough backwards to make a navel shape. Re-roll the trimmings and repeat until all the dough is used up.

4 Bring a pan of lightly salted water to the boil over a medium heat. Add the tortellini, in batches, and cook for 5 minutes. Drain and transfer to a large serving dish.

5 To make the sauce, put the cream and garlic into a pan and bring to the boil over a low heat. Simmer for 3 minutes. Add the mushrooms and half the Parmesan cheese, season and simmer for 2–3 minutes. Pour the sauce over the tortellini, sprinkle over the remaining Parmesan cheese, garnish with the parsley and serve.

chicken with orange sauce

serves four

2 tbsp rapeseed oil

2 tbsp olive oil

4 x 225 g/8 oz chicken suprêmes

150 ml/5 fl oz brandy

2 tbsp plain flour

150 ml/5 fl oz freshly squeezed
   orange juice

25 g/1 oz courgette, cut into
   thin batons

25 g/1 oz red pepper, cut into
   thin batons

25 g/1 oz leek, shredded finely

400 g/14 oz dried
   wholemeal spaghetti

3 large oranges, peeled and cut
   into segments

rind of 1 orange, cut into very
   fine strips

2 tbsp chopped fresh tarragon

150 ml/5 fl oz fromage frais or
   ricotta cheese

salt and pepper

fresh tarragon leaves, to garnish

1 Heat the rapeseed oil and
1 tablespoon of the olive oil in a
frying pan over a fairly high heat. Add
the chicken and cook until golden. Add
the brandy and cook for 3 minutes.
Sprinkle in the flour and cook, stirring
constantly, for 2 minutes.

2 Reduce the heat and add the
orange juice, courgette, red
pepper and leek. Season to taste with
salt and pepper. Simmer for 5 minutes
until the sauce has thickened.

3 Meanwhile, bring a pan of lightly
salted water to the boil over a
medium heat. Add the pasta and cook
for 10 minutes, or until tender, but still
firm to the bite. Drain the pasta,
transfer to a warmed serving dish and
drizzle over the remaining oil.

4 Add half the orange segments,
half the orange rind, the tarragon
and fromage frais or ricotta cheese to
the sauce in the pan and cook for
3 minutes.

5 Put the chicken on top of the
pasta, pour over a little sauce,
garnish with the remaining orange
segments, rind and tarragon. Serve
immediately with any extra sauce.

filipino chicken

serves four

1 can lemonade or lime-
  and-lemonade

2 tbsp gin

4 tbsp tomato ketchup

2 tsp garlic salt

2 tsp Worcestershire sauce

4 lean chicken suprêmes or
  breast fillets

salt and pepper

TO SERVE

cooked thread egg noodles

1 fresh green chilli, chopped finely

2 spring onions, sliced

1 Mix the lemonade or lime-and-lemonade, gin, tomato ketchup, garlic salt and Worcestershire sauce together in a large, non-porous dish. Season to taste with salt and pepper.

2 Put the chicken into the dish and pour over the gin mixture, ensuring that the chicken is completely covered.

3 Leave the chicken to marinate in the refrigerator for 2 hours, then remove and leave, covered, at room temperature for 30 minutes.

4 Put the chicken over a medium-hot barbecue and cook for 20 minutes, turning the chicken once, halfway through the cooking time.

5 Remove the cooked chicken from the barbecue and leave to rest for 3–4 minutes before serving.

6 Serve with cooked egg noodles, tossed with a little green chilli and spring onions.

breast of pheasant lasagne

serves four

225 g/8 oz pork fat, diced

2 tbsp butter

16 small onions

8 large pheasant breasts, sliced

2½ tbsp plain flour

600 ml/1 pint chicken stock

1 bouquet garni

450 g/1 lb fresh peas, shelled

1 tbsp butter for greasing

14 sheets precooked lasagne

850 ml/1½ pints Béchamel Sauce
    (see page 98)

75 g/2¾ oz mozzarella cheese

fresh parsley leaves, to garnish

salt

TO SERVE

cooked baby onions

cooked peas

1 Bring a large pan of lightly salted water to the boil over a medium heat. Add the pork fat and simmer for 3 minutes, then drain and pat dry on kitchen paper.

2 Melt the butter in a large frying pan over a low heat. Add the pork fat and onions to the pan and cook, stirring occasionally, for about 3 minutes or until lightly browned.

3 Remove the pork fat and onions from the pan and reserve. Add the pheasant slices and cook over a low heat for 12 minutes until browned all over. Transfer to an ovenproof dish.

4 Stir the flour into the pan and cook until just brown. Blend in the stock, then pour over the pheasant. Add the bouquet garni and cook in a preheated oven at 200°C/400°F/ Gas Mark 6, for 5 minutes. Remove the bouquet garni. Add the onions, pork fat and peas and return to the oven for about 10 minutes.

5 Put the pheasant and pork fat into a food processor and chop finely.

6 Reduce the oven temperature to 190°C/375°F/Gas Mark 5. Grease an ovenproof dish with butter. Layer lasagne, pheasant sauce and Béchamel Sauce (see page 98) in the dish, ending with the Béchamel Sauce. Sprinkle over the cheese and bake for 35 minutes or until golden. Garnish with parsley and serve with baby onions and peas.

braised garlic chicken

serves four

4 garlic cloves, chopped

4 shallots, chopped

2 small fresh red chillies, deseeded
   and chopped

1 lemon grass stalk, chopped finely

1 tbsp chopped fresh coriander

1 tsp shrimp paste

½ tsp ground cinnamon

1 tbsp tamarind paste

2 tbsp vegetable oil

8 small chicken joints, such as
   drumsticks or thighs

300 ml/10 fl oz chicken stock

1 tbsp Thai fish sauce

1 tbsp smooth peanut butter

4 tbsp toasted peanuts, chopped

salt and pepper

TO SERVE

stir-fried vegetables

boiled noodles

1 Put the garlic, shallots, chillies, lemon grass, coriander and shrimp paste into a mortar and pound with a pestle to an almost smooth paste. Stir in the cinnamon and tamarind paste.

2 Heat the oil in a wide frying pan over a medium heat. Add the chicken joints, turning frequently, until golden brown on all sides. Remove from the pan and keep hot. Tip away any excess fat.

3 Add the garlic paste to the pan and cook over a medium heat, stirring constantly, until lightly browned. Stir in the stock and return the chicken to the pan.

4 Bring to the boil over a medium heat. Cover, reduce the heat and simmer, stirring occasionally, for about 25–30 minutes, or until the chicken is tender and cooked through. Stir in the fish sauce and peanut butter and simmer gently for a further 10 minutes.

5 Season to taste with salt and pepper and sprinkle the toasted peanuts over the chicken. Serve with a selection of stir-fried vegetables and boiled noodles.

chicken with vegetables

4 part boned chicken breasts

2 tbsp olive oil

25 g/1 oz butter

1 large onion, chopped finely

2 garlic cloves, crushed

2 peppers, deseeded and cut
    into large pieces

225 g/8 oz large closed cup
    mushrooms, sliced or quartered

175 g/6 oz tomatoes, peeled
    and halved

150 ml/5 fl oz dry white wine

125–175 g/4–6 oz stoned
    green olives

4–6 tbsp double cream

salt and pepper

350 g/12 oz freshly cooked pasta

chopped fresh parsley, to garnish

1 Season the chicken with salt and
    pepper. Heat the oil and butter in
a frying pan over a medium heat. Add
the chicken and fry until browned.
Remove the chicken from the pan.

2 Add the onion and garlic and fry
    gently until starting to soften. Add
the peppers and mushrooms and cook
for a few minutes longer.

3 Add the tomatoes and plenty of
    seasoning, then transfer the
vegetable mixture to a large ovenproof
casserole. Put the chicken on to the
bed of vegetables.

4 Add the wine to the frying pan
    and bring to the boil over a
medium heat. Pour the wine over the
chicken and cover tightly. Cook in a
preheated oven at 180°C/350°F/
Gas Mark 4, for 50 minutes.

5 Add the olives to the chicken, mix
    lightly, then pour on the cream.
Re-cover the casserole and return to
the oven for 10–20 minutes, or until
the chicken is very tender.

6 Adjust the seasoning and transfer
    the chicken, vegetables and sauce
to a serving plate with freshly cooked
pasta. Garnish with chopped parsley
and serve immediately.

slices of duck with pasta

serves four

4 x 275 g/9½ oz boned breasts
    of duckling
25 g/1 oz butter
55 g/2 oz finely chopped carrots
55 g/2 oz finely chopped shallots
1 tbsp lemon juice
150 ml/5 fl oz meat stock
4 tbsp clear honey
115 g/4 oz fresh or thawed
    frozen raspberries
25 g/1 oz plain flour
1 tbsp Worcestershire sauce
400 g/14 oz fresh linguine
salt and pepper
TO GARNISH
fresh raspberries
1 fresh flat-leaf parsley sprig

1 Trim and score the duck breasts with a knife and season. Melt the butter in a pan over a low heat. Add the duck and fry until lightly coloured.

2 Add the carrots, shallots, lemon juice and half the stock and simmer over a low heat for 1 minute. Stir in half the honey and half the raspberries. Sprinkle over half the flour and cook, stirring constantly, for 3 minutes. Season with pepper to taste and add the Worcestershire sauce.

3 Stir in the remaining stock and cook for 1 minute. Stir in the remaining honey and remaining raspberries and sprinkle over the remaining flour. Cook for 3 minutes.

4 Remove the duck breasts from the pan, but leave the sauce to simmer over a very low heat.

5 Meanwhile, bring a large pan of lightly salted water to the boil over a medium heat. Add the linguine and cook until tender, but still firm to the bite. Drain and transfer to 4 warmed serving plates.

6 Slice the duck breast lengthways into 5-mm/¼-inch thick pieces. Pour a little sauce over the pasta and arrange the sliced duck in a fan shape on top of it. Garnish with fresh raspberries and parsley and serve.

Fish & Seafood

Pasta is a natural partner for fish and seafood. Both are cooked quickly to preserve their flavour and texture, they are packed full of nutritional goodness and the varieties available are almost infinite. The superb recipes in this chapter demonstrate the full range of these qualities. For a quick, easy and satisfying supper, try Fish & Vegetable Lasagne, Red Mullet Fillets with Orecchiette, Mixed Seafood & Leek Lasagne or Vermicelli with Clams. More unusual and sophisticated dishes include Sea Bass with Macaroni & Olive Sauce, Poached Salmon with Penne, Ravioli of Lemon Sole & Haddock and Farfallini with Buttered Lobster.

steamed pasta pudding

115 g/4 oz dried short-cut macaroni
    or other short pasta

15 g/½ oz butter, plus extra
    for greasing

450 g/1 lb white fish fillets, such as
    cod or haddock

2–3 fresh parsley sprigs

6 black peppercorns

125 ml/4 fl oz double cream

2 eggs, separated

2 tbsp chopped fresh dill or parsley

pinch of freshly grated nutmeg

55 g/2 oz freshly grated
    Parmesan cheese

salt and pepper

fresh dill sprigs, to garnish

Tomato Sauce, to serve
    (see page 126)

1 Bring a pan of lightly salted water to the boil over a medium heat. Add the pasta and cook until tender, but still firm to the bite. Drain the pasta, return to the pan, add the butter, cover and keep warm.

2 Put the fish in a frying pan. Add the parsley, peppercorns and enough water to cover. Bring to the boil over a medium heat, cover and simmer for 10 minutes. Lift out the fish and cool. Reserve the cooking liquid.

3 Skin the fish and cut into bite-sized pieces. Put the pasta into a bowl. Mix the cream, egg yolks, chopped dill, nutmeg and Parmesan cheese together, pour into the pasta and mix. Spoon in the fish. Add enough of the reserved cooking liquid to make a moist, but firm mixture. Whisk the egg whites until stiff, then fold into the mixture.

4 Grease a heatproof bowl and spoon in the fish mixture to within 4 cm/1½ inches of the rim. Cover with greased greaseproof paper and tinfoil and tie securely with string.

5 Stand the bowl on a trivet in a pan. Add enough boiling water to reach halfway up the sides. Cover and steam for 1½ hours.

6 Invert the pudding on to a plate. Pour over a little Tomato Sauce (see page 126). Garnish with fresh dill and serve with the remaining sauce.

baked seafood & macaroni with fennel

serves four

350 g/12 oz dried short-cut
macaroni

1 tbsp olive oil, plus extra for
brushing

85 g/3 oz butter, plus extra for
greasing

2 small fennel bulbs, thinly sliced
and fronds reserved

175 g/6 oz mushrooms, thinly sliced

175 g/6 oz peeled, cooked prawns

pinch of cayenne pepper

300 ml/10 fl oz Béchamel Sauce
(see Cook's Tip, right)

55 g/2 oz freshly grated Parmesan
cheese

2 large tomatoes, sliced

1 tsp dried oregano

salt and pepper

1 Bring a saucepan of salted water
to the boil. Add the pasta and oil
and cook until tender, but still firm to
the bite. Drain and return to the pan.
Add 25 g/1 oz of butter, cover, shake
the pan and keep the pasta warm.

2 Melt the remaining butter in a
saucepan. Fry the fennel for 3–4
minutes. Stir in the mushrooms and fry
for a further 2 minutes. Stir in the
prawns, then remove from the heat.

3 Stir the cayenne pepper and
prawn mixture into the Béchamel
sauce. Pour into a greased ovenproof
dish and spread evenly. Sprinkle over
the Parmesan cheese and arrange the
tomato slices in a ring around the
edge. Brush the tomatoes with olive oil
and sprinkle over the oregano.

4 Bake in a preheated oven at
180°C/350°F/Gas Mark 4 for 25
minutes, or until golden brown. Serve
immediately.

COOK'S TIP

For Béchamel sauce, melt 25 g/ 1
oz butter. Stir in 25 g/1 oz flour.
Cook, stirring, for 2 minutes.
Gradually, stir in 300 ml/10 fl oz
warm milk. Add 2 tbsp finely
chopped onion, 5 white
peppercorns and 2 parsley sprigs
and season with salt, dried
thyme and grated nutmeg.
Simmer, stirring, for 15 minutes.
Strain before using.

trout with smoked bacon

serves four

1 tbsp butter for greasing

4 whole trout, 275 g/9½ oz each,
    gutted and cleaned

12 canned anchovy fillets in oil,
    drained and chopped

2 apples, peeled, cored and sliced

4 fresh mint sprigs

juice of 1 lemon

12 slices rindless smoked
    streaky bacon

450 g/1 lb dried tagliatelle

salt and pepper

TO GARNISH

2 apples, cored and sliced

4 fresh mint sprigs

1 Grease a deep baking tray with the butter.

2 Open up the cavities of each trout and rinse with warm salt water.

3 Season each cavity with salt and pepper. Divide the anchovies, sliced apples and mint sprigs between each of the cavities. Sprinkle with lemon juice.

4 Carefully cover the whole of each trout, except the head and tail, with 3 slices of smoked bacon in a spiral shape.

5 Arrange the trout on the baking tray with the loose ends of bacon tucked underneath. Season with pepper and bake in a preheated oven at 200°C/400°F/Gas Mark 6, for 20 minutes, turning the trout over after 10 minutes.

6 Meanwhile, bring a large pan of lightly salted water to the boil over a medium heat. Add the pasta and cook for about 12 minutes, or until tender, but still firm to the bite. Drain the pasta and transfer to 4 large, warmed serving plates.

7 Remove the trout from the oven and arrange on the pasta. Garnish with sliced apples and fresh mint sprigs and serve immediately.

sea bass with macaroni & olive sauce

serves four

25 g/1 oz butter

4 shallots, chopped

2 tbsp capers

175 g/6 oz stoned green
 olives, chopped

4 tbsp balsamic vinegar

300 ml/10 fl oz fish stock

300 ml/10 fl oz double cream

juice of 1 lemon

450 g/1 lb dried macaroni

8 x 115 g/4 oz sea bass medallions

salt and pepper

mixture of lemon slices, shredded
 leek and shredded carrot,
 to garnish

1 To make the sauce, melt the butter in a frying pan over a low heat. Add the shallots and cook for 4 minutes. Add the capers and olives and cook for a further 3 minutes.

2 Stir in the balsamic vinegar and the stock, bring to the boil over a low heat and reduce by half. Add the cream, stirring, and reduce again by half. Season to taste with salt and pepper and stir in the lemon juice. Remove from the heat and keep warm.

3 Bring a large pan of lightly salted water to the boil over a medium heat. Add the pasta and cook for about 12 minutes, or until tender, but still firm to the bite.

4 Cook the sea bass medallions under a preheated hot grill for 3–4 minutes on each side, until cooked through, do not overcook.

5 Drain the pasta and transfer to 4 large, warmed serving dishes. Top the pasta with the fish and pour over the olive sauce. Garnish with lemon slices, shredded leek and shredded carrot and serve immediately.

spaghetti al tonno

serves four

200 g/7 oz canned tuna, drained

55 g/2 oz canned anchovy
    fillets, drained

225 ml/8 fl oz olive oil

55 g/2 oz roughly chopped
    flat-leaf parsley

150 ml/5 fl oz crème fraîche

450 g/1 lb dried spaghetti

25 g/1 oz butter

salt and pepper

TO GARNISH

black olives

4 fresh flat-leaf parsley sprigs

1 Remove any bones from the tuna, then put into a food processor or blender, together with the anchovies, 225 ml/8 fl oz of the oil and the chopped parsley. Process until the mixture is smooth.

2 Using a spoon, add the crème fraîche to the food processor or blender and process again for a few seconds to blend thoroughly. Season to taste with salt and pepper.

3 Bring a large pan of lightly salted water to the boil over a medium heat. Add the pasta and cook until tender, but still firm to the bite.

4 Drain the pasta, return to the pan and put over a medium heat. Add the butter and toss well to coat. Spoon in the sauce and, using 2 forks, quickly toss into the pasta.

5 Remove the pan from the heat and transfer the pasta to 4 large, warmed serving plates. Garnish with olives and fresh parsley sprigs and serve immediately.

red mullet fillets with orecchiette

serves four

85 g/3 oz plain flour

8 red mullet fillets

25 g/1 oz butter

150 ml/5 fl oz fish stock

1 tbsp crushed almonds

1 tsp pink peppercorns

1 orange, peeled and cut
   into segments

1 tbsp orange liqueur

grated rind of 1 orange

450 g/1 lb dried orecchiette

150 ml/5 fl oz double cream

4 tbsp amaretto

salt and pepper

TO GARNISH:

2 tbsp snipped fresh chives

1 tbsp toasted slivered almonds

1 Season the flour with salt and pepper and sprinkle into a shallow bowl. Press the fish fillets into the flour to coat. Melt the butter in a large frying pan over a low heat. Add the fish fillets and fry for 3 minutes or until browned.

2 Add the stock to the pan and cook for 4 minutes. Carefully transfer the fish to a heatproof plate, cover with tinfoil and keep warm.

3 Add the almonds, pink peppercorns, half the orange segments, the orange liqueur and orange rind to the pan. Simmer until the liquid has reduced by half.

4 Meanwhile, bring a large pan of lightly salted water to the boil over a medium heat. Add the pasta and cook for 15 minutes, or until tender, but still firm to the bite.

5 Meanwhile, season the sauce with salt and pepper and stir in the cream and amaretto. Cook for 2 minutes. Return the fish fillets to the pan to coat with the sauce.

6 Drain the pasta and transfer to a serving dish. Top with the fish fillets and the sauce. Garnish with the remaining orange segments, chives and toasted almonds. Serve.

squid & macaroni stew

serves four

225 g/8 oz dried short-cut macaroni
  or other small pasta shapes

6 tbsp olive oil

2 onions, sliced

350 g/12 oz prepared squid, cut
  into 4-cm/1½-inch strips

225 ml/8 fl oz fish stock

150 ml/5 fl oz red wine

350 g/12 oz tomatoes, peeled and
  sliced thinly

2 tbsp tomato purée

1 tsp dried oregano

2 bay leaves

2 tbsp chopped fresh parsley

salt and pepper

1 Bring a large pan of lightly salted water to the boil over a medium heat. Add the macaroni and cook for about 3 minutes. Drain, return to the pan, cover and keep warm.

2 Heat the oil in a pan over a medium heat. Add the onions and fry until translucent. Add the squid and stock and simmer for about 5 minutes. Pour in the wine and add the tomatoes, tomato purée, oregano and bay leaves. Bring the sauce to the boil, season and cook for 5 minutes.

3 Stir the macaroni into the pan, cover and simmer for 10 minutes, or until the squid and macaroni are tender and the sauce has thickened.

If the sauce remains too runny, uncover the pan and continue cooking for a few more minutes.

4 Remove the bay leaves and discard. Reserve a little parsley and stir the remainder into the pan. Transfer to a warmed serving dish and sprinkle over the remaining parsley. Serve immediately.

noodles with prawns

serves four

225 g/8 oz dried thin egg noodles

2 tbsp peanut oil

1 garlic clove, crushed

½ tsp ground star anise

1 bunch spring onions, cut into
    5-cm/2-inch pieces

24 raw tiger prawns, peeled with
    tails intact

2 tbsp light soy sauce

2 tsp lime juice

lime wedges, to garnish

1 Bring a large pan of water to the boil over a medium heat. Add the noodles and blanch for 2 minutes.

2 Drain the noodles well, rinse under cold running water and drain thoroughly again. Keep warm and reserve until required.

3 Heat a large wok, add the peanut oil and heat until almost smoking.

4 When the oil is hot, add the garlic and ground star anise and stir-fry for about 30 seconds.

5 Add the spring onions and tiger prawns and stir-fry for 3 minutes.

6 Stir in the light soy sauce, lime juice and noodles and mix well.

7 Cook the mixture in the wok for about 1 minute until thoroughly heated through and all the ingredients are completely incorporated.

8 Spoon the noodle and prawn mixture into a warmed serving dish. Transfer to serving bowls, garnish with lime wedges and serve.

poached salmon with penne

serves four

4 x 275 g/9½ oz fresh salmon steaks

85 g/3 oz butter

175 ml/6 fl oz dry white wine

pinch of sea salt

8 peppercorns

1 fresh dill sprig

1 fresh tarragon sprig

1 lemon, sliced

450 g/1 lb dried penne

2 tbsp olive oil

25 g/1 oz plain flour

150 ml/5 fl oz warm milk

juice and finely grated rind of
  2 lemons

55 g/2 oz chopped watercress

salt and pepper

TO GARNISH

lemon slices

fresh watercress

1 Put the salmon into a large frying pan. Add 55 g/2 oz of the butter, the wine, sea salt, peppercorns, dill, tarragon and lemon slices. Bring to the boil over a medium heat, cover and simmer for 10 minutes.

2 Using a fish slice, carefully remove the salmon. Strain and reserve the cooking liquid. Remove the salmon skin and centre bones and discard. Put into a warmed dish, cover and keep warm.

3 Bring a large pan of lightly salted water to the boil over a medium heat. Add the pasta and cook for about 12 minutes, or until tender, but still firm to the bite. Drain and sprinkle with the oil. Put into a warmed serving dish, top with the salmon and keep warm.

4 Melt the remaining butter in a pan over a low heat and stir in the flour for 2 minutes. Stir in the milk and 7 tablespoons of the cooking liquid. Add the lemon juice and rind and cook, stirring, for 10 minutes.

5 Add the watercress to the sauce, stir gently and season to taste with salt and pepper.

6 Pour the sauce over the salmon and garnish with lemon slices and watercress. Serve immediately.

salmon lasagne rolls

serves four

8 sheets green lasagne

1 onion, sliced

15 g/½ oz butter

½ red pepper, chopped

1 courgette, diced

1 tsp chopped fresh root ginger

125 g/4½ oz oyster mushrooms,
    preferably yellow,
    chopped coarsely

225 g/8 oz fresh salmon fillet,
    skinned and cut into chunks

2 tbsp dry sherry

2 tsp cornflour

20 g/¾ oz plain flour

20 g/¾ oz butter

300 ml/ 10 fl oz milk

25 g/1 oz freshly grated
    Cheddar cheese

15 g/½ oz fresh white breadcrumbs

salt and pepper

mixed salad leaves, to serve

1 Put the lasagne sheets into a large shallow dish. Cover with plenty of boiling water. Cook in the microwave on HIGH for 5 minutes. Leave to stand, covered, for a few minutes before draining. Rinse in cold water and lay the sheets out on a clean work surface.

2 Put the onion and butter into a bowl. Cover and cook on HIGH for 2 minutes. Add the red pepper, courgette and ginger. Cover and cook on HIGH for 3 minutes.

3 Add the mushrooms and salmon to the bowl. Mix the sherry into the cornflour, then stir into the bowl. Cover and cook on HIGH for 4 minutes until the fish flakes when tested with a fork. Season to taste with salt and pepper.

4 Whisk the flour, butter and milk together in a bowl. Cook on HIGH for 3–4 minutes, whisking every minute, to give a sauce of coating consistency. Stir in half the cheese and season with salt and pepper.

5 Spoon the salmon filling in equal quantities along the shorter side of each lasagne sheet. Roll up to enclose the filling. Arrange in a lightly greased large rectangular dish. Pour over the sauce and sprinkle over the remaining cheese and the breadcrumbs.

6 Cook on HIGH for 3 minutes until heated through. If possible, lightly brown under a preheated hot grill before serving. Transfer to 4 large, warmed serving plates and serve immediately with salad.

ravioli of lemon sole & haddock

serves four

450 g/1 lb lemon sole
fillets, skinned

450 g/1 lb haddock fillets, skinned

3 eggs, beaten

450 g/1 lb cooked potato gnocchi

175 g/6 oz fresh breadcrumbs

3 tbsp double cream

450 g/1 lb Homemade Pasta Dough
(see page 50)

300 ml 10 fl oz Italian Red Wine
Sauce (see page 96)

55 g/2 oz freshly grated
Parmesan cheese

salt and pepper

COOK'S TIP

When making square ravioli,
divide the dough into two. Wrap
half in clingfilm and cover with a
damp tea towel. Roll out the
other half thinly and spoon in the
filling at regular intervals. Brush
the spaces in between with
water. Roll out the second dough
and lift into position. Press the
edges firmly to seal. Cut out with
a ravioli cutter or knife.

1 Flake the lemon sole and haddock fillets with a fork and transfer the flesh to a large mixing bowl.

2 Mix the eggs, cooked potato gnocchi, breadcrumbs and cream together in a bowl until thoroughly mixed. Add the fish to the bowl containing the gnocchi and season to taste with salt and pepper.

3 Roll out the Pasta Dough (see page 50) on to a floured work surface and cut out 7.5-cm/3-inch rounds using a plain cutter.

4 Put a spoonful of the fish filling on each round. Dampen the edges slightly and fold the pasta rounds over, pressing together to seal.

5 Bring a large pan of lightly salted water to the boil over a medium heat. Add the ravioli and cook for 2–4 minutes or until cooked through.

6 Using a slotted spoon, drain the ravioli and transfer to a large serving dish. Pour over the Italian Red Wine Sauce (see page 96), sprinkle over Parmesan cheese and serve.

linguine with sardines

serves four

8 sardines, filleted

1 fennel bulb

4 tbsp olive oil

3 garlic cloves, sliced

1 tsp crushed chillies

350 g/12 oz dried linguine

½ tsp finely grated lemon rind

1 tbsp lemon juice

2 tbsp pine kernels, toasted

2 tbsp chopped fresh parsley

salt and pepper

1 Wash the sardine fillets and pat dry on kitchen paper. Roughly chop them into large pieces and reserve. Trim the fennel bulb, discard the outer leaves and slice very thinly.

2 Heat 2 tablespoons of the oil in a large frying pan over a medium-high heat and add the garlic and chillies. Cook for 1 minute, then add the fennel slices. Cook, stirring occasionally, for 4–5 minutes until softened. Reduce the heat, add the sardine pieces and cook for a further 3–4 minutes until just cooked.

3 Meanwhile, bring a large pan of lightly salted water to the boil over a medium heat. Add the pasta and cook for 8–10 minutes, or until tender, but still firm to the bite. Drain thoroughly and return to the pan.

4 Add the lemon rind, lemon juice, pine kernels and parsley to the sardines and toss together. Season to taste with salt and pepper. Add to the pasta with the remaining oil and toss together gently. Transfer to a warmed serving dish and serve immediately.

vermicelli with clams

serves four

400 g/14 oz dried vermicelli,
   spaghetti or other long pasta

25 g/1 oz butter

1 tbsp olive oil

2 onions, chopped

2 garlic cloves, chopped

400 g/14 oz bottled clams in brine

125 ml/4 fl oz white wine

4 tbsp chopped fresh parsley

½ tsp dried oregano

pepper

pinch of freshly grated nutmeg

TO GARNISH

2 tbsp Parmesan cheese shavings

fresh basil sprigs

1 Bring a large pan of lightly salted water to the boil over a medium heat. Add the pasta and cook until tender, but still firm to the bite. Drain, thoroughly, return to the pan and add the butter. Cover the pan, shake well and keep warm.

2 Heat the oil in a pan over a medium heat. Add the onions and fry until translucent. Stir in the garlic and cook for 1 minute.

3 Strain the liquid from the bottled clams into bowl. Add half of it to the pan with the white wine and discard the remaining liquid. Stir, then bring to simmering point and simmer for 3 minutes.

4 Add the clams, parsley and oregano to the pan and season with pepper and nutmeg. Reduce the heat and cook until heated through.

5 Transfer the pasta to a warmed serving dish and pour over the sauce. Garnish with shavings of Parmesan cheese and basil sprigs. Serve immediately.

corsican clam spaghetti

serves four

400 g/14 oz fresh spaghetti

salt

CORSICAN CLAM SAUCE

900 g/2 lb live clams

4 tbsp olive oil

3 large garlic cloves, crushed

pinch of crushed chillies, optional

900 g/2 lb tomatoes, peeled and
 chopped, with juice reserved

55 g/2 oz stoned green or black
 olives, chopped

1 tbsp chopped fresh oregano or
 ½ tsp dried oregano

1 To make the sauce, put the clams into a bowl of lightly salted water and leave to soak for 30 minutes. Rinse them under cold running water and scrub lightly to remove any sand from the shells.

2 Discard any broken clams or open clams that refuse to close when firmly tapped. This indicates they are dead and can cause food poisoning, if eaten. Leave the clams to soak in a large bowl of water. Meanwhile, bring a large pan of lightly salted water to the boil over a medium heat.

3 Heat the oil in a large frying pan over a medium heat. Add the garlic and chillies (if using) and fry, stirring constantly, for about 2 minutes.

4 Stir in the tomatoes, olives and oregano. Reduce the heat and simmer, stirring frequently, until the tomatoes soften and start to break up. Cover and simmer for 10 minutes.

5 Meanwhile, add the pasta to the large pan of boiling water and cook for about 8–10 minutes, or until tender, but still firm to the bite. Drain

thoroughly, reserving 125 ml/4 fl oz of the cooking liquid. Return the pasta to the pan and keep warm.

6 Add the clams and reserved cooking liquid to the sauce and stir. Bring to the boil, stirring constantly. Discard any clams that have not opened and transfer the sauce to a larger pan.

7 Add the pasta to the sauce and toss until well coated, then transfer to 4 large, warmed serving dishes. Serve immediately.

pasta with broccoli & anchovy sauce

serves four

500 g/1 lb 2 oz broccoli

400 g/14 oz dried orecchiette

5 tbsp olive oil

2 large garlic cloves, crushed

50 g/1¾ oz canned anchovy fillets in
oil, drained and chopped finely

55 g/2 oz fresh Parmesan cheese

55 g/2 oz fresh pecorino cheese

salt and pepper

1 Bring 2 pans of lightly salted water to the boil over a medium heat. Chop the broccoli florets and stems into small, bite-sized pieces. Add the broccoli to 1 pan and cook until very tender. Drain and reserve.

2 Put the pasta in the other pan of boiling water and cook for 10–12 minutes, or until tender, but still firm to the bite

3 Meanwhile, heat the oil in a large pan over a medium heat. Add the garlic and fry for 3 minutes, stirring, without allowing it to brown. Add the chopped anchovies and cook for 3 minutes, stirring and mashing with a wooden spoon to break them up. Finely grate the Parmesan and pecorino cheeses on separate plates.

4 Drain the pasta, add to the pan of anchovies and stir. Add the broccoli and stir to mix.

5 Add the grated Parmesan and pecorino cheeses to the pasta and stir constantly over a medium-high heat until the cheeses melt and the pasta and broccoli are coated.

6 Adjust the seasoning to taste – the anchovies and cheeses are salty, so you will only need to add pepper. Transfer to 4 warmed bowls and serve immediately.

pan-fried prawns

serves four

4 garlic cloves

20–24 large, raw prawns, unpeeled

125 g/4½ oz butter

4 tbsp olive oil

6 tbsp brandy

2 tbsp chopped fresh parsley

salt and pepper

350 g/12 oz freshly cooked pasta,
   to serve

1 Peel and slice the garlic with a sharp knife.

2 Wash the prawns under cold running water and pat dry on kitchen paper.

3 Melt the butter with the oil in a large frying pan over a high heat. Add the garlic and prawns and fry, stirring constantly, for 3–4 minutes, or until the prawns turn pink.

4 Sprinkle with brandy and season to taste with salt and pepper and sprinkle with chopped parsley. Transfer to 4 large, warmed plates and serve immediately with freshly cooked pasta.

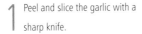

165

spaghetti al vongole

serves four

900 g/2 lb live clams

2 tbsp olive oil

1 large onion, chopped finely

2 garlic cloves, chopped finely

1 tsp fresh thyme leaves

150 ml/5 fl oz white wine

400 g/14 oz canned
    chopped tomatoes

350 g/12 oz dried spaghetti

1 tbsp chopped fresh parsley

salt and pepper

4 fresh thyme sprigs, to garnish

COOK'S TIP

If you are able to get only
very large clams, reserve a few
in their shells to garnish and
shell the rest.

1 Soak the clams in salted water for 30 minutes. Rinse in cold water and scrub lightly. Discard any broken or open clams and put into a pan with just the water clinging to their shells. Cook, covered, over a high heat for 3–4 minutes until opened. Remove from the heat and strain, reserving any liquid. Discard any that remain closed.

2 Heat the oil in a pan over a low heat. Add the onion and cook for 10 minutes, or until softened, but not coloured. Add the garlic and thyme and cook for a further 30 seconds.

3 Increase the heat and add the white wine. Simmer rapidly until reduced and syrupy. Add the tomatoes and reserved clam liquid. Cover and simmer for 15 minutes. Uncover and simmer for a further 15 minutes or until thickened. Season to taste with salt and pepper.

4 Meanwhile, bring a large pan of lightly salted water to the boil over a medium heat. Add the pasta and cook for 8–10 minutes, or until tender, but still firm to the bite. Drain thoroughly and return to the pan.

5 Add the clams to the tomato sauce and heat through for 2–3 minutes. Add the parsley and stir. Add the sauce to the pasta and mix. Transfer to 4 warmed serving bowls and garnish with thyme sprigs. Serve.

farfalle with a medley of seafood

serves four

12 raw tiger prawns

12 raw prawns

125 g/4½ oz freshwater prawns

450 g/1 lb fillet of sea bream

55 g/2 oz butter

12 scallops, shelled

juice and finely grated rind of
　1 lemon

pinch of saffron powder or threads

1 litre/1¾ pints vegetable stock

150 ml/5 fl oz rose-petal vinegar
　(See page 109)

450 g/1 lb dried farfalle

150 ml/5 fl oz white wine

1 tbsp pink peppercorns

115 g/4 oz baby carrots

150 ml/5 fl oz double cream or
　fromage frais

salt and pepper

1 fresh flat-leaf parsley sprig,
　to garnish

1 Using a sharp knife, peel and devein the prawns and thinly slice the sea bream. Melt the butter in a large pan over a low heat, add all the seafood and cook for 1–2 minutes.

2 Season with pepper and add the lemon juice and grated rind. Very carefully add a pinch of saffron powder or a few strands of saffron to the cooking juices (not to the seafood).

3 Remove the seafood from the pan, reserve and keep warm.

4 Return the pan to the heat and add the stock. Bring to the boil over a medium heat and reduce by one third. Add the rose petal vinegar and cook for 4 minutes or until reduced.

5 Bring a pan of lightly salted water to the boil over a medium heat. Add the farfalle and cook until tender, but still firm to the bite. Drain the pasta thoroughly, transfer to a large, warmed serving plate and top with the seafood.

6 Add the wine, peppercorns and carrots to the pan and reduce the sauce for 6 minutes. Add the cream, then simmer for 2 minutes.

7 Pour the sauce over the seafood and pasta and garnish with a parsley sprig. Serve immediately.

farfallini buttered lobster

serves four

2 x 700 g/1 lb 9 oz lobsters, split
    into halves
juice and grated rind of 1 lemon
115 g/4 oz butter
4 tbsp fresh white breadcrumbs
2 tbsp brandy
5 tbsp double cream or
    crème fraîche
350 g/12 oz dried farfallini
55 g/2 oz freshly grated
    Parmesan cheese
salt and pepper
TO GARNISH
1 kiwi fruit, sliced
4 cooked king prawns, unpeeled
fresh dill sprigs

1 Carefully discard the stomach sac, vein and gills from each lobster. Remove all the meat from the tail and chop. Crack the legs, remove the meat and chop. Transfer the meat to a large bowl and add the lemon juice and grated lemon rind.

2 Clean the shells thoroughly and put into a preheated oven at 160°C/325°/Gas Mark 3 to dry out.

3 Melt 25 g/1 oz of the butter in a frying pan over a low heat. Add the breadcrumbs and fry for 3 minutes, or until crisp and golden brown.

4 Melt the remaining butter in a pan over a low heat. Add the lobster meat and heat through gently. Add the brandy and cook for a further 3 minutes, then add the cream or crème fraîche and season to taste with salt and pepper.

5 Meanwhile, bring a large pan of lightly salted water to the boil over a medium heat. Add the pasta and cook for 12 minutes, or until tender, but still firm to the bite. Drain and spoon the pasta into the clean shells. Top with the buttered lobster and sprinkle with a little Parmesan cheese and the breadcrumbs. Cook under a preheated hot grill for about 2–3 minutes or until golden brown.

6 Transfer the lobster shells to a large, warmed serving dish, garnish with the kiwi fruit, king prawns and dill sprigs and serve immediately.

thai noodles

serves four

350 g/12 oz cooked, peeled
   tiger prawns
115 g/4 oz flat rice noodles or
   rice vermicelli
4 tbsp vegetable oil
2 garlic cloves, chopped finely
1 egg
2 tbsp lemon juice
4½ tsp Thai fish sauce
½ tsp sugar
2 tbsp roasted peanuts, chopped
½ tsp cayenne pepper
2 spring onions, cut into
   2.5-cm/1-inch pieces
55 g/2 oz bean sprouts
1 tbsp chopped fresh coriander

1 Drain the tiger prawns on kitchen paper to remove excess moisture. Reserve. Cook the rice noodles according to the packet instructions. Drain well and reserve until required.

2 Heat a large wok over a high heat. Add the oil and when hot, add the garlic. Cook, stirring constantly, until just golden. Add the egg and stir quickly to break it up. Cook for a few seconds.

3 Add the prawns and noodles, scraping down the sides of the wok to ensure they mix with the egg and garlic.

4 Add the lemon juice, fish sauce, sugar, half the peanuts, cayenne pepper, spring onions and half the bean sprouts stirring quickly all the time. Cook over a high heat for a further 2 minutes until heated through.

5 Transfer to a large warmed serving plate. Top with the remaining peanuts and bean sprouts and sprinkle with the chopped coriander. Serve immediately.

sesame noodles with prawns

serves four

1 garlic clove, chopped

1 spring onion, chopped

1 small fresh red chilli, deseeded
   and sliced

1 tbsp chopped fresh coriander

300 g/10½ oz dried fine egg noodles

2 tbsp vegetable oil

2 tsp sesame oil

1 tsp shrimp paste

225 g/8 oz raw, prawns peeled

2 tbsp lime juice

2 tbsp Thai fish sauce

1 tsp sesame seeds, toasted

1 Put the garlic, spring onion, chilli
   and coriander into a mortar and
grind with a pestle to a smooth paste.

2 Bring a large pan of water to the
   boil over a medium heat. Add the
noodles and cook for 4 minutes, or
according to the packet instructions.

3 Heat a large wok over a medium
   heat. Add the vegetable and
sesame oils and when hot, stir in the
shrimp paste and ground coriander
mixture. Stir for 1 minute.

4 Stir in the prawns and stir-fry for
   2 minutes. Stir in the lime juice
and fish sauce, then cook for 1 minute.

5 Drain the noodles and toss
   them into the wok. Transfer to
4 warmed bowls and sprinkle with the
sesame seeds. Serve immediately.

spaghetti & shellfish

225 g/8 oz dried spaghetti, broken
  into 15-cm/6-inch lengths

2 tbsp olive oil

300 ml/10 fl oz fish or chicken stock

1 tsp lemon juice

1 small cauliflower, cut into florets

2 carrots, sliced thinly

115 g/4 oz mangetout

55 g/2 oz butter

1 onion, sliced

225 g/8 oz courgettes, sliced

1 garlic clove, chopped

350 g/12 oz cooked, peeled
  prawns, thawed if frozen

2 tbsp chopped fresh parsley

25 g/1 oz freshly grated
  Parmesan cheese

½ tsp paprika

salt and pepper

4 cooked, unpeeled prawns,
  to garnish

crusty bread, to serve

1 Bring a pan of lightly salted water to the boil over a medium heat. Add the pasta and cook until tender, but still firm to the bite. Drain the pasta thoroughly and return to the pan. Using 2 forks, toss the pasta with the oil, then cover and keep warm.

2 Bring the stock and lemon juice to the boil over a medium heat. Add the cauliflower and carrots and cook for 3–4 minutes. Remove from the pan and reserve. Add the mangetout to the pan and cook for 1–2 minutes. Reserve with the other vegetables.

3 Melt half the butter in a frying pan over a medium heat. Add the onion and courgettes and fry for about 3 minutes. Add the garlic and prawns and cook for a further 2–3 minutes, until completely heated through.

4 Stir in the reserved vegetables and heat through. Season to taste with salt and pepper and stir in the remaining butter.

5 Transfer the pasta to a large, serving dish. Pour over the sauce and add the parsley. Using 2 forks, toss until the pasta is coated. Sprinkle over the Parmesan cheese and paprika, garnish with the prawns and serve immediately with crusty bread.

sicilian pasta

serves four

6 tbsp olive oil

55 g/2 oz fresh white breadcrumbs

450 g/1 lb broccoli, cut into
  small florets

350 g/12 oz dried tagliatelle

4 canned anchovy fillets, drained
  and chopped

2 garlic cloves, sliced

grated rind of 1 lemon

large pinch of crushed chillies

salt and pepper

freshly grated Parmesan cheese,
  to serve

1 Heat 2 tablespoons of the oil in a frying pan over a medium heat. Add the breadcrumbs and stir-fry for 4–5 minutes until golden and crisp. Drain on kitchen paper.

2 Bring a large pan of lightly salted water to the boil over a medium heat. Add the broccoli and blanch for 3 minutes, then drain, reserving the water. Refresh the broccoli under cold running water and drain again. Pat dry on kitchen paper and reserve.

3 Bring the water back to the boil and add the pasta and cook for 8–10 minutes, or until tender, but still firm to the bite.

4 Meanwhile, heat 2 tablespoons of the remaining oil in a large frying pan over a low heat. Add the anchovies and cook for 1 minute, then mash with a wooden spoon to a paste. Add the garlic, lemon rind and chillies and cook gently for 2 minutes. Add the broccoli and cook for a further 3–4 minutes or until heated through.

5 Drain the cooked pasta and mix with the broccoli mixture and the remaining oil. Season to taste with salt and pepper. Toss together well.

6 Transfer the pasta to 4 large, warmed serving plates. Top with the fried breadcrumbs and Parmesan cheese and serve immediately.

pasta puttanesca

serves four

3 tbsp extra virgin olive oil

1 large red onion, chopped finely

4 canned anchovy fillets, drained

pinch of crushed chillies

2 garlic cloves, chopped finely

400 g/14 oz canned tomatoes

2 tbsp tomato purée

225 g/8 oz dried spaghetti

25 g/1 oz stoned black olives,
    chopped roughly

25 g/1 oz stoned green olives,
    chopped roughly

1 tbsp capers, rinsed and drained

4 sun-dried tomatoes in oil, drained
    and chopped roughly

salt and pepper

fresh herb sprigs, to garnish

1 Heat the oil in a frying pan over a low heat. Add the onion, anchovies and chillies and cook for 10 minutes until softened. Add the garlic and cook for 30 seconds. Stir in the tomatoes and tomato purée, Bring to the boil and simmer for 10 minutes.

2 Meanwhile, bring a large pan of lightly salted water to the boil over a medium heat. Add the pasta and cook for 8–10 minutes, or until tender, but still firm to the bite.

3 Add the olives, capers and sun-dried tomatoes to the sauce. Simmer for a further 2–3 minutes. Season to taste with salt and pepper.

4 Drain the pasta well and stir in the sauce. Toss thoroughly to mix. Transfer to a warmed serving dish and garnish with fresh herbs. Serve.

saffron mussel tagliatelle

serves four

1 kg/2 lb 4 oz mussels

150 ml/5 fl oz white wine

1 medium onion, chopped finely

25 g/1 oz butter

2 garlic cloves, crushed

2 tsp cornflour

300 ml/10 fl oz double cream

pinch of saffron threads or
    saffron powder

1 egg yolk

juice of ½ lemon

450 g/1 lb dried tagliatelle

salt and pepper

3 tbsp chopped fresh parsley,
    to garnish

1 Pull the 'beards' off the mussels and scrub in cold water. Discard any that refuse to close when sharply tapped. Put the wine and onion into a large pan and bring to the boil over a high heat. Add the mussels, cover and cook, shaking the pan frequently, for 4–6 minutes or until the shells open.

2 Drain and reserve the cooking liquid. Discard any mussels that remain closed. Reserve a few mussels for the garnish and remove the remainder from their shells.

3 Strain the cooking liquid into a pan. Bring to the boil over a medium heat and reduce by about half. Remove the pan from the heat.

4 Melt the butter in a pan over a low heat. Add the garlic and cook, stirring frequently, for 2 minutes, until golden. Stir in the cornflour and cook, stirring, for 1 minute. Gradually stir in the cooking liquid and the cream. Crush the saffron threads and add to the pan. Season to taste with salt and pepper and simmer for 2–3 minutes until thickened.

5 Stir in the egg yolk, lemon juice and shelled mussels. Do not allow the mixture to boil.

6 Bring a pan of lightly salted water to the boil over a medium heat. Add the pasta and cook until tender, but still firm to the bite. Drain and transfer to a serving dish. Add the mussel sauce and toss. Garnish with parsley and reserved mussels. Serve.

pasta shells with mussels

serves four–six

1.25 kg/2 lb 12 oz mussels
225 ml/8 fl oz dry white wine
2 large onions, chopped
115 g/4 oz unsalted butter
6 large garlic cloves, chopped finely
5 tbsp chopped fresh parsley
300 ml/10 fl oz double cream
400 g/14 oz dried pasta shells
salt and pepper
crusty bread, to serve

1 Pull the 'beards' off the mussels and scrub in cold water. Discard any that refuse to close when sharply tapped. Put the wine and 1 of the onions into a large pan and bring to the boil over a high heat. Add the mussels, cover and cook, shaking the pan frequently, for about 4–6 minutes, or until the shells open.

2 Remove the pan from the heat. Drain the mussels and reserve the cooking liquid. Discard any mussels that remain closed. Strain the cooking liquid through a clean cloth into a glass jug or bowl and reserve.

3 Melt the butter in a pan over a medium heat. Add the remaining onion and fry until translucent. Stir in the garlic and cook for 1 minute. Gradually stir in the reserved cooking liquid. Stir in the parsley and cream and season to taste with salt and pepper. Bring to simmering point over a low heat.

COOK'S TIP

Pasta shells are ideal because the sauce collects in the cavities and impregnates the pasta with flavour.

4 Meanwhile, bring a large pan of lightly salted water to the boil over a medium heat. Add the pasta and cook until tender, but still firm to the bite. Drain thoroughly, return to the pan, cover and keep warm.

5 Reserve a few mussels for the garnish and remove the remainder from their shells. Stir the shelled mussels into the cream sauce and warm briefly.

6 Transfer the pasta to a large, warmed serving dish. Pour over the sauce and toss well to coat. Garnish with the reserved mussels and serve immediately with crusty bread.

spaghettini with crab

serves four

1 dressed crab, about 450 g/1 lb
    including the shell
350 g/12 oz dried spaghettini
6 tbsp extra virgin olive oil
1 fresh red chilli, deseeded and
    chopped finely
2 garlic cloves, chopped finely
3 tbsp chopped fresh parsley
2 tbsp lemon juice
1 tsp finely grated lemon rind
salt and pepper
lemon wedges, to garnish

COOK'S TIP
If you prefer to buy your
own fresh crab you will need
a large crab weighing about
1 kg/2 lb 4 oz.

1 Using a sharp knife, scoop the meat from the crab shell into a bowl. Mix the white and brown meat together lightly and reserve.

2 Bring a large pan of lightly salted water to the boil over a medium heat. Add the pasta and cook for 8–10 minutes, or until tender, but still firm to the bite. Drain thoroughly and return to the pan.

3 Meanwhile, heat 2 tablespoons of the oil in a frying pan over a low heat. Add the chilli and garlic and cook for 30 seconds, then add the crabmeat, chopped parsley, lemon juice and rind. Stir-fry for 1 minute until the crab is just heated through.

4 Add the crab mixture to the pasta with the remaining oil and season to taste with salt and pepper. Toss together thoroughly and transfer to a large, warmed serving dish and garnish with a few lemon wedges. Serve immediately.

neapolitan salad

serves four

450 g/1 lb prepared squid, cut
   into strips

750 g/1 lb 10 oz cooked mussels

450 g/1 lb cooked cockles in
   brine, drained

150 ml/5 fl oz white wine

300 ml/10 fl oz olive oil

225 g/8 oz dried campanelle or
   other small pasta shapes

juice of 1 lemon

1 bunch fresh chives, snipped

1 bunch fresh parsley,
   chopped finely

4 large tomatoes

mixed salad leaves

salt and pepper

1 fresh basil sprig, to garnish

1 Put all the seafood into a large
   bowl, pour over the wine and half
the oil, then leave for 6 hours.

2 Put the seafood mixture into a
   pan and simmer over a low heat
for 10 minutes. Leave to cool.

3 Bring a large pan of lightly salted
   water to the boil over a medium
heat. Add the pasta and and cook until
tender, but still firm to the bite. Drain
thoroughly and refresh in cold water.

4 Strain off about half of the cooking
   liquid from the seafood and discard
the rest. Mix in the lemon juice, chives,
parsley and the remaining oil. Season
to taste with salt and pepper. Drain the
pasta and add to the seafood.

5 Cut the tomatoes into quarters.
   Shred the salad leaves and
arrange them at the base of a salad
bowl. Spoon in the seafood salad and
garnish with the quartered tomatoes
and a basil sprig. Serve.

VARIATION

You can substitute cooked
scallops for the mussels and also
clams in brine for the cockles.

pasta vongole

serves four

675 g/1 lb 8 oz live clams or 280 g/
10 oz canned clams, drained

2 tbsp olive oil

2 garlic cloves, chopped finely

400 g/14 oz raw mixed seafood,
such as squid and mussels,
cleaned or thawed if frozen

150 ml/5 fl oz white wine

150 ml/5 fl oz fish stock

675 g/1 lb 8 oz fresh pasta or
350 g/12 oz dried pasta

2 tbsp chopped fresh tarragon

salt and pepper

VARIATION

Red clam sauce can be made by
adding 8 tbsp of passata to the
sauce along with the fish stock in
step 4. Follow the same cooking
method as in main recipe.

1 If you are using live clams, scrub
them clean and discard any that
are already open.

2 Heat the oil in a large frying pan
over a medium heat. Add the
garlic and clams, cover and cook for
2 minutes, shaking the pan to ensure
that the clams are coated in the oil.

3 Add the remaining seafood
mixture to the pan and cook for
a further 2 minutes.

4 Pour the wine and stock over the
mixed seafood and garlic and
bring to the boil over a medium heat.
Cover the pan, reduce the heat and
simmer for 8–10 minutes, or until the
shells open. Discard any clams or
mussels that remain closed.

5 Meanwhile, bring a large pan of
lightly salted water to the boil.
Add the pasta and cook until tender,
but still firm to the bite. Drain well.

6 Stir the chopped tarragon into the
sauce and season to taste with
salt and pepper.

7 Transfer the pasta to 4 large,
warmed serving plates and pour
over the sauce. Serve immediately.

singapore noodles

serves four

225 g/8 oz dried egg noodles

6 tbsp vegetable oil

4 eggs, beaten

3 garlic cloves, crushed

1½ tsp chilli powder

225 g/8 oz skinless, boneless
    chicken, cut into thin strips

3 celery sticks, sliced

1 green pepper, deseeded
    and sliced

4 spring onions, sliced

25 g/1 oz water
    chestnuts, quartered

2 fresh red chillies, sliced

300 g/10½ oz cooked,
    peeled prawns

175 g/6 oz bean sprouts

2 tsp sesame oil

COOK'S TIP

When mixing precooked
ingredients into the dish, such as
the egg and noodles, ensure that
they are heated right through
and are hot when ready to serve.

1 Soak the noodles in boiling water for 4 minutes or until soft. Leave to drain on kitchen paper.

2 Heat a wok over a high heat. Add 2 tablespoons of the oil and when hot, add the eggs. Stir until set. Carefully remove the cooked eggs from the wok, reserve and keep warm.

3 Add the remaining oil to the wok. Add the garlic and chilli powder and stir-fry for 30 seconds.

4 Add the chicken strips and stir-fry for 4–5 minutes or until starting to brown.

5 Stir in the celery, green pepper, spring onions, water chestnuts and chillies and cook for a further 8 minutes, or until the chicken is completely cooked through.

6 Add the prawns and the reserved noodles to the wok, together with the bean sprouts and toss to mix well.

7 Break the cooked egg with a fork and sprinkle it over the noodles, then sprinkle the sesame oil over the noodles. Serve immediately.

Vegetable Pasta

The pasta recipes in this chapter offer something special for every occasion: filling vegetarian suppers, unusual vegetable side dishes, main course and side salads. You could even take many of the salads on a picnic and, of course, they are perfect as accompaniments for summer barbecues. Some are classic dishes, such as Traditional Cannelloni, Pesto Pasta and Spaghetti with Peas & Cream. Others are imaginative and sometimes surprising new combinations of vegetables and pasta. Try Artichoke & Olive Pasta, Spinach & Wild Mushroom Lasagne, Vegetable Ravioli and Three-Cheese Macaroni for a family meal, or Fried Vegetable Noodles as a side dish.

pasta with nuts & cheese

serves four

55 g/2 oz pine kernels

350 g/12 oz dried pasta shapes

125 g/4½ oz broccoli, broken
    into florets

2 courgettes, sliced

200 g/7 oz full-fat soft cheese

150 ml/5 fl oz milk

1 tbsp chopped fresh basil

125 g/4½ oz button
    mushrooms, sliced

85 g/3 oz blue cheese, crumbled

salt and pepper

4 fresh basil sprigs, to garnish

green salad, to serve

1 Scatter the pine kernels on to a baking tray and cook under a preheated hot grill, turning occasionally, until lightly browned. Reserve.

2 Bring a pan of salted water to the boil over a medium heat. Add the pasta and cook for 8–10 minutes, or until tender, but still firm to the bite.

3 Bring a pan of lightly salted water to the boil over a medium heat. Add the broccoli and courgettes and cook for 5 minutes or until just tender.

4 Put the soft cheese into a pan and heat over a low heat, stirring. Add the milk and stir. Add the basil and mushrooms and cook for about 2–3 minutes. Stir the blue cheese into the mixture and season to taste.

5 Drain the pasta and the vegetables and mix together. Pour the cheese and mushroom sauce over them and add the pine kernels, tossing the pasta gently to mix them in. Transfer to 4 serving dishes, garnish with basil sprigs and serve with a green salad.

tricolour pasta

serves four

450 g/1 lb dried farfalle

450 g/1 lb cherry tomatoes

85 g/3 oz rocket

salt and pepper

4 tbsp olive oil

fresh pecorino cheese, to garnish

1 Bring a large pan of lightly salted water to the boil over a medium heat. Add the pasta and cook for about 8–10 minutes, or until tender, but still firm to the bite. Drain the pasta thoroughly and return to the pan.

2 Cut the cherry tomatoes in half and trim the rocket.

3 Heat the oil in a large frying pan. Add the halved tomatoes and cook for 1 minute. Add the pasta and the rocket and stir gently to mix. Heat through and season to taste with salt and pepper.

4 Meanwhile, using a vegetable peeler, shave thin slices of pecorino cheese.

5 Transfer the pasta and vegetables to a warmed serving dish and garnish with the pecorino cheese shavings. Serve immediately.

COOK'S TIP

Pecorino cheese is a hard sheep's milk cheese, which resembles Parmesan and is often used for grating over a variety of dishes. It has a sharp flavour and is used only in small quantities.

tagliatelle & garlic sauce

serves four

2 tbsp walnut oil

1 bunch spring onions, sliced

2 garlic cloves, sliced thinly

225 g/8 oz mushrooms, sliced

500 g/1 lb 2 oz fresh green and
white tagliatelle

225 g/8 oz frozen chopped leaf
spinach, thawed and drained

125 g/4½ oz full-fat soft cheese
with garlic and herbs

4 tbsp single cream

55 g/2 oz chopped, unsalted
pistachio nuts

2 tbsp shredded fresh basil

salt and pepper

4 fresh basil sprigs, to garnish

Italian bread, to serve

1 Gently heat the oil in a frying pan
over a low heat. Add the spring
onions and garlic and fry for 1 minute
or until softened. Add the mushrooms
to the pan, stir well, cover and cook
gently for 5 minutes or until softened.

2 Meanwhile, bring a large pan of
lightly salted water to the boil
over a medium heat and cook the
pasta for 3–5 minutes, or until just
tender, but still firm to the bite. Drain
thoroughly and return to the pan.

3 Add the spinach to the
mushrooms and heat through for
1–2 minutes. Add the cheese and
allow to melt slightly. Stir in the cream
and continue to heat without allowing
it to boil.

4 Pour the vegetable mixture over
the pasta, season to taste with
salt and pepper and mix well. Heat
gently, stirring, for 2–3 minutes.

5 Transfer the pasta into a warmed
serving bowl and sprinkle over
the pistachio nuts and shredded basil.
Garnish with fresh basil sprigs and
serve with Italian bread.

pasta & chilli tomatoes

275 g/9½ oz dried pappardelle

3 tbsp groundnut oil

2 garlic cloves, crushed

2 shallots, sliced

225 g/8 oz green beans, sliced

100 g/3½ oz cherry
   tomatoes, halved

1 tsp crushed chillies

4 tbsp crunchy peanut butter

150 ml/5 fl oz coconut milk

1 tbsp tomato purée

VARIATION

Add slices of chicken or beef to
the recipe and stir-fry with the
beans and pasta in step 3 for a
more substantial main meal.

---

1 Bring a large pan of lightly salted water to the boil over a medium heat. Add the pasta and cook for about 8–10 minutes, or until tender, but still firm to the bite. Drain well and reserve.

2 Meanwhile, heat a large wok over a high heat. Add the oil and when hot, add the garlic and shallots and stir-fry for 1 minute.

3 Add the green beans and drained pasta to the wok and stir-fry for 5 minutes. Add the cherry tomatoes and mix well.

4 Mix the chillies, peanut butter, coconut milk and tomato purée together in a small bowl. Pour the chilli mixture into the wok, toss well and heat through.

5 Transfer to a warmed serving dish and serve immediately.

vegetable ravioli

serves four

450 g/1 lb Homemade Pasta Dough
   (see page 50)
6 tbsp butter
150 ml/5 fl oz single cream
85 g/3 oz freshly grated
   Parmesan cheese
1 fresh basil sprig, to garnish
FILLING
2 large aubergines
3 large courgettes
6 large tomatoes
1 large green pepper
1 large red pepper
3 garlic cloves
1 large onion
125 ml/4 fl oz olive oil
4½ tsp tomato purée
½ tsp chopped fresh basil
salt and pepper

1 To make the filling, cut the aubergines and the courgettes into 2.5-cm/1-inch chunks. Layer the aubergine pieces in a colander, sprinkle each layer with salt and leave for about 20 minutes. Rinse and drain, then pat dry on kitchen paper.

2 Blanch the tomatoes in boiling water for 2 minutes. Drain, peel and chop the flesh. Core and deseed the peppers and cut into 2.5-cm/1-inch dice. Chop the garlic and onion.

3 Heat the oil in a large pan over a low heat. Add the garlic and onion and fry, stirring occasionally, for 3 minutes.

4 Stir in the aubergines, courgettes, tomatoes, peppers, tomato purée and chopped basil. Season to taste with salt and pepper, cover and simmer for 20 minutes, stirring frequently.

5 Roll out the Pasta Dough (see page 50) and cut out 7.5-cm/ 3-inch rounds with a plain cutter. Put a spoonful of the filling on each round. Dampen the edges slightly and fold the rounds over, pressing together to seal.

6 Bring a large pan of lightly salted water to the boil over a medium heat. Add the ravioli and cook for about 3–4 minutes. Drain and transfer to a greased ovenproof dish, dotting each layer with butter. Pour over the cream and sprinkle over the Parmesan cheese. Bake in a preheated oven at 200°C/400°F/Gas Mark 6, for 20 minutes. Garnish with a basil sprig and serve immediately.

summertime tagliatelle

serves four

650 g/1 lb 7 oz courgettes

6 tbsp olive oil

3 garlic cloves, crushed

3 tbsp chopped fresh basil

2 fresh red chillies, deseeded
   and sliced

juice of 1 large lemon

5 tbsp single cream

4 tbsp freshly grated
   Parmesan cheese

225 g/8 oz dried tagliatelle

salt and pepper

COOK'S TIP

Lime juice could be used instead
of the lemon. As limes are
usually smaller, squeeze the juice
from 2 fruits.

1 Using a swivel vegetable peeler,
slice the courgettes into very
thin ribbons.

2 Heat the oil in a frying pan over
a low heat. Add the garlic and
cook for 30 seconds.

3 Add the courgette ribbons and
cook, stirring constantly, for
3–5 minutes. Stir in the basil, chillies,
lemon juice, cream and Parmesan
cheese. Season to taste with salt and
pepper. Keep warm over a low heat.

4 Meanwhile, bring a large pan of
lightly salted water to the boil
over a medium heat. Add the pasta
and cook for 8–10 minutes, or until
tender, but still firm to the bite. Drain
thoroughly and put the pasta in a
large, warmed serving bowl.

5 Pile the courgette mixture on top
of the pasta. Serve immediately.

artichoke & olive spaghetti

serves four

2 tbsp olive oil

1 large red onion, cut into wedges

2 garlic cloves, crushed

1 tbsp lemon juice

4 baby aubergines, quartered

600 ml/1 pint passata

2 tsp caster sugar

2 tbsp tomato purée

400 g/14 oz canned artichoke
    hearts, drained and halved

115 g/4 oz stoned black olives

350 g/12 oz wholewheat
    dried spaghetti

salt and pepper

4 fresh basil sprigs, to garnish

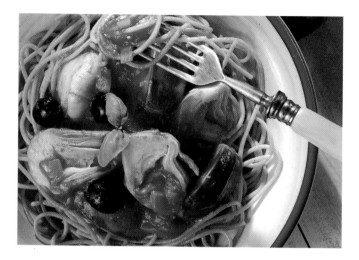

2 Pour in the passata, season to taste with salt and pepper and stir in the sugar and tomato purée. Bring to the boil over a medium heat, reduce the heat and simmer for 20 minutes.

3 Gently stir in the artichoke hearts and olives and cook for about 5 minutes.

1 Heat 1 tablespoon of the oil in a large frying pan over a low heat. Add the onion, garlic, lemon juice and aubergines and cook for 4–5 minutes, or until lightly browned.

4 Meanwhile, bring a large pan of lightly salted water to the boil over a medium heat. Add the pasta and cook for 8–10 minutes, or until tender, but still firm to the bite. Drain, toss in the remaining oil and season.

5 Transfer the spaghetti to 4 large, warmed serving bowls and top with the vegetable sauce. Garnish with basil sprigs and serve immediately.

beetroot cannolicchi

serves four

300 g/10½ oz dried ditalini rigati

4 tbsp olive oil

2 garlic cloves, chopped

400 g/14 oz canned
   chopped tomatoes

400 g/14 oz cooked beetroot, diced

2 tbsp chopped fresh basil leaves

1 tsp mustard seeds

salt and pepper

TO SERVE

mixed salad leaves, tossed in
   olive oil

4 Italian plum tomatoes, sliced

1 Bring a large pan of lightly salted water to the boil over a medium heat. Add the pasta and cook for about 8–10 minutes, or until tender, but still firm to the bite. Drain well and reserve.

2 Heat the oil in a large pan. Add the garlic and fry for 3 minutes. Add the chopped tomatoes and cook for 10 minutes.

3 Remove the pan from the heat and carefully add the beetroot, basil, mustard seeds and pasta and season to taste with salt and pepper.

4 Serve on a bed of mixed salad leaves tossed in olive oil and sliced plum tomatoes.

chilli & pepper pasta

serves four

2 red peppers, halved
  and deseeded

1 small fresh red chilli

2 garlic cloves

4 tomatoes, halved

50 g/1¾ oz ground almonds

7 tbsp olive oil

675 g/1 lb 8 oz fresh pasta or
  350 g/12 oz dried pasta

fresh oregano leaves, to garnish

1 Put the peppers, skin-side up, on to a baking tray with the chilli, garlic and tomatoes, skin-side down. Cook under a preheated hot grill until charred. After 10 minutes, turn the tomatoes skin-side up.

2 Put the peppers and chillies into a plastic bag and leave to sweat for 10 minutes.

3 Remove the skin from the peppers and deseed and skin the chillies. Slice the flesh into strips.

4 Peel the garlic and peel and deseed the tomatoes.

5 Put the almonds on to a baking tray and put under the grill for 2–3 minutes or until golden.

VARIATION

Add 2 tbsp of red wine vinegar to the sauce and use as a dressing for a cold pasta salad, if you prefer.

6 Put the pepper, chilli, garlic and tomatoes into a food processor and process until a purée forms. Keep the motor running and slowly add the oil to form a thick sauce. Alternatively, mash the mixture with a fork and beat in the oil, drop by drop.

7 Stir the toasted ground almonds into the mixture.

8 Put the sauce into a pan and warm until it is heated through.

9 Bring a pan of lightly salted water to the boil over a medium heat. Add the pasta and cook until tender, but still firm to the bite. Drain and transfer to 4 large serving dishes. Pour over the sauce and toss to mix. Garnish with fresh oregano leaves and serve.

pesto pasta

225 g/8 oz chestnut
   mushrooms, sliced
150 ml/5 fl oz vegetable stock
175 g/6 oz asparagus, trimmed and
   cut into 5-cm/2-inch lengths
300 g/10½ oz fresh green and
   white tagliatelle
400 g/14 oz canned artichoke
   hearts, drained and halved
breadsticks, to serve
PESTO
2 large garlic cloves, crushed
15 g/½ oz fresh basil leaves
6 tbsp low-fat natural fromage frais
2 tbsp freshly grated
   Parmesan cheese
salt and pepper
TO GARNISH
shredded fresh basil leaves
fresh Parmesan cheese shavings

1 Put the mushrooms into a pan
with the stock. Bring to the boil
over a low heat, cover and simmer for
3–4 minutes or until just tender. Drain
and reserve, reserving the cooking
liquid to use in soups if you wish.

2 Bring a small pan of water to the
boil over a medium heat. Add the
asparagus and cook for 3–4 minutes
until just tender. Drain and reserve.

3 Bring a large pan of lightly salted
water to the boil over a medium
heat. Add the pasta and cook until
tender, but still firm to the bite. Drain
the pasta thoroughly, return to the pan
and keep warm.

4 Meanwhile, to make the pesto,
put all the ingredients into a food
processor or blender and process for a
few seconds until a smooth purée
forms. Alternatively, finely chop the
basil, then mix all the ingredients
together in a small bowl.

5 Add the mushrooms, asparagus
and artichoke hearts to the pasta
and cook, stirring constantly, over a

low heat for 2–3 minutes. Remove
from the heat and mix with the pesto.

6 Transfer to 4 large warmed bowls
and garnish with fresh basil and
shavings of Parmesan cheese. Serve.

spaghetti & mushroom sauce

serves four

55 g/2 oz butter

1 tbsp olive oil

6 shallots, sliced

450 g/1 lb sliced button mushrooms

1 tsp plain flour

150 ml/5 fl oz double cream

2 tbsp port

115 g/4 oz sun-dried
    tomatoes, chopped

freshly grated nutmeg

450 g /1 lb dried spaghetti

1 tbsp chopped fresh parsley

salt and pepper

1 fresh parsley sprig, to garnish

6 triangles of fried white bread,
    to serve

1 Heat the butter and 1 tablespoon of the oil in a pan over a medium heat. Add the shallots and cook for 3 minutes. Add the mushrooms and cook for 2 minutes. Season, then stir in the flour and cook for 1 minute.

2 Gradually stir in the cream and port, add the sun-dried tomatoes and a pinch of grated nutmeg and cook over a low heat for 8 minutes.

3 Meanwhile, bring a large pan of lightly salted water to the boil over a medium heat. Add the pasta and cook for about 12–14 minutes, or until tender, but still firm to the bite.

VARIATION

Non-vegetarians could add
115 g/4 oz Parma ham, cut
into thin strips and heated gently
in 25 g/1 oz butter, to the pasta
along with the mushroom sauce.

4 Drain the pasta and return to the pan. Pour over the mushroom sauce and cook for 3 minutes. Transfer to a large serving plate and sprinkle over the chopped parsley. Garnish with a parsley sprig and serve with crispy triangles of fried bread.

paglia e fieno

serves four

55 g/2 oz butter

900 g/2 lb fresh peas, shelled

200 ml/7 fl oz double cream

450 g/1 lb fresh green and white
   spaghetti or tagliatelle

55 g/2 oz freshly grated Parmesan

pinch of freshly grated nutmeg

salt and pepper

fresh Parmesan cheese shavings,
   to serve

VARIATION

Fry 140 g/5 oz sliced button or
oyster mushrooms in 55 g/2 oz
butter over a low heat for about
4–5 minutes. Stir into the peas
and cream sauce just before
adding to the pasta in step 4.

1 Melt the butter in a large pan over a low heat. Add the peas and cook for 2–3 minutes.

2 Using a measuring jug, pour 150 ml/5 fl oz of the cream into the pan, bring to the boil over a low heat and simmer for 1–1½ minutes or until slightly thickened. Remove the pan from the heat.

3 Meanwhile, bring a large pan of lightly salted water to the boil over a medium heat. Add the pasta and cook for 2–3 minutes, or until tender, but still firm to the bite. Remove from the heat, drain the pasta thoroughly and return to the pan.

4 Add the peas and cream sauce to the pasta and return the pan to the heat. Add the remaining cream and the Parmesan cheese, then season to taste with salt, pepper and freshly grated nutmeg.

5 Gently toss the pasta with 2 forks to coat with the peas and cream sauce, while heating through.

6 Transfer the pasta to 4 warmed serving dishes and serve with shavings of Parmesan cheese.

pasta with green vegetables

serves four

225 g/8 oz dried gemelli or other
   pasta shapes
1 head broccoli, cut into florets
2 courgettes, sliced
225 g/8 oz asparagus spears
115 g/4 oz mangetout
115 g/4 oz frozen peas
25 g/1 oz butter
3 tbsp vegetable stock
4 tbsp double cream
freshly grated nutmeg
2 tbsp chopped fresh parsley
2 tbsp fresh Parmesan
   cheese shavings
salt and pepper

1 Bring a large pan of lightly salted water to the boil over a medium heat. Add the pasta and cook until tender, but still firm to the bite. Drain, return to the pan and keep warm.

2 Steam the broccoli, courgettes, asparagus and mangetout over a pan of boiling water until starting to soften. Remove from the heat and refresh in cold water. Drain and reserve.

3 Bring a small pan of lightly salted water to the boil over a low heat. Add the frozen peas and cook for 3 minutes. Drain the peas, refresh in cold water, then drain again. Reserve with the other vegetables.

4 Put the butter and vegetable stock into a pan over a medium heat. Add all of the vegetables, reserving a few of the asparagus spears, and toss carefully with a wooden spoon until they have heated through, taking care not to break them up.

5 Stir in the cream and heat through without bringing to the boil. Season to taste with salt, pepper and freshly grated nutmeg.

6 Transfer the pasta to a warmed serving dish and stir in the chopped parsley. Spoon over the vegetable sauce and sprinkle over the Parmesan cheese. Arrange the reserved asparagus spears in a pattern on top and serve.

italian tomato sauce & pasta

serves two

1 tbsp olive oil

1 small onion, chopped finely

1–2 garlic cloves, crushed

350 g/12 oz tomatoes, peeled
  and chopped

2 tsp tomato purée

2 tbsp water

300–350 g/10½–12 oz dried
  pasta shapes

85 g/3 oz lean bacon, derinded
  and diced

40 g/1½ oz mushrooms, sliced

1 tbsp chopped fresh parsley or
  1 tsp chopped fresh coriander

2 tbsp soured cream or natural
  fromage frais, optional

salt and pepper

1 To make the sauce, heat the oil in
a pan over a low heat. Add the
onion and garlic and fry until soft.

2 Add the tomatoes, tomato purée,
and water to the pan. Season to
taste with salt and pepper and bring to
the boil. Cover and simmer gently for
10 minutes.

3 Meanwhile, bring a pan of lightly
salted water to the boil over a
medium heat. Add the pasta and cook
for 8–10 minutes, or until tender, but
still firm to the bite. Drain and transfer
to 2 warmed serving dishes.

4 Heat the bacon gently in a large
frying pan until the fat runs,
then add the mushrooms and continue
cooking for about 3–4 minutes. Drain
off any excess oil.

5 Add the bacon and mushrooms to
the tomato mixture, together with
the parsley or coriander and the soured
cream or fromage frais (if using). Heat
through and serve with the pasta.

COOK'S TIP

Soured cream contains 18–20%
fat, so if you are following a
low-fat diet you can leave it out
of this recipe or substitute a
low-fat alternative.

pasta & bean casserole

serves four

225 g/8 oz dried haricot beans,
    soaked overnight and drained

225 g/8 oz dried penne

850 ml/1½ pints vegetable stock

5 tbsp olive oil

2 large onions, sliced

2 garlic cloves, chopped

2 bay leaves

1 tsp dried oregano

1 tsp dried thyme

5 tbsp red wine

2 tbsp tomato purée

2 celery sticks, sliced

1 fennel bulb, sliced

115 g/4 oz sliced mushrooms

225 g/8 oz tomatoes, sliced

1 tsp dark muscovado sugar

4 tbsp dry white breadcrumbs

salt and pepper

TO SERVE

salad leaves

crusty bread

1 Put the haricot beans into a large pan and pour over enough cold water to cover. Bring to the boil over a high heat and boil rapidly for 20 minutes. Drain and keep warm.

2 Bring a large pan of lightly salted water to the boil over a medium heat. Add the pasta and cook for about 3 minutes, or until almost tender. Drain thoroughly and keep warm.

3 Put the beans into a large, ovenproof casserole dish. Add the stock and stir in the oil, the onions, garlic, bay leaves, oregano, thyme, wine and tomato purée. Bring to the boil over a medium heat, then cover and cook in a preheated oven at 180ºC/350ºF/Gas Mark 4, for 2 hours.

4 Add the pasta, celery, fennel, mushrooms and tomatoes to the casserole dish and season with salt and pepper. Stir in the muscovado sugar, then sprinkle over the breadcrumbs. Cover the dish and cook in the oven for 1 further hour.

5 Transfer to 4 serving dishes and serve with salad and bread.

spinach & wild mushroom lasagne

serves four

115 g/4 oz butter, plus extra
    for greasing
2 garlic cloves, chopped finely
115 g/4 oz shallots
225 g/8 oz wild mushrooms
450 g/1 lb spinach, cooked, drained
    and chopped finely
225 g/8 oz freshly grated
    Cheddar cheese
¼ tsp freshly grated nutmeg
1 tsp chopped fresh basil
55 g/2 oz plain flour
600 ml/1 pint hot milk
55 g/2 oz freshly grated
    Cheshire cheese
salt and pepper
8 sheets precooked lasagne

1 Lightly grease an ovenproof dish with a little butter.

2 Melt 55 g/2 oz of the butter in a pan over a low heat. Add the garlic, shallots and wild mushrooms and fry for 3 minutes. Stir in the spinach, Cheddar cheese, nutmeg and chopped basil. Season well with salt and pepper and reserve.

3 Melt the remaining butter in another pan over a low heat. Add the flour and cook, stirring constantly, for 1 minute. Gradually stir in the hot milk, whisking constantly until smooth. Stir in 25 g/1 oz of the Cheshire cheese and season to taste.

4 Spread half of the mushroom and spinach mixture over the base of the prepared dish. Cover with a layer of lasagne, then with half the cheese sauce. Repeat the process and sprinkle over the remaining Cheshire cheese. Bake the lasagne in a preheated oven at 200°C/400°F/Gas Mark 6, for 30 minutes, or until golden brown. Transfer to 4 serving plates and serve.

penne & vegetables

serves four

225 g/8 oz dried penne

2 tbsp olive oil

2 tbsp butter

2 garlic cloves, crushed

1 green pepper, deseeded and
    sliced thinly

1 yellow pepper, deseeded and
    sliced thinly

16 cherry tomatoes, halved

1 tbsp chopped fresh oregano

125 ml/4 fl oz dry white wine

2 tbsp quartered, stoned
    black olives

75 g/2¾ oz rocket

salt and pepper

fresh oregano sprigs, to garnish

1 Bring a large pan of lightly salted water to the boil over a medium heat. Add the pasta and cook for 8–10 minutes, or until tender, but still firm to the bite. Drain thoroughly.

2 Heat the oil and butter gently in a frying pan. Add the garlic and fry for 30 seconds, then add the peppers and cook for 3–4 minutes.

3 Stir in the cherry tomatoes, oregano, wine and olives and cook for about 3–4 minutes. Season to taste with salt and pepper and stir in the rocket until just wilted.

4 Transfer to a serving dish, spoon over the sauce and garnish with oregano sprigs. Serve.

VARIATION

If rocket is unavailable, spinach makes a good substitute. Follow the same cooking instructions as for the rocket.

vegetables & tofu

serves four

225 g/8 oz asparagus

115 g/4 oz mangetout

225 g/8 oz French beans

1 leek

225 g/8 oz shelled small
    broad beans

300 g/10½ oz dried fusilli

2 tbsp olive oil

2 tbsp butter or margarine

1 garlic clove, crushed

225 g/8 oz tofu, cut into 2.5-cm/
    1-inch cubes (drained weight)

55 g/2 oz stoned green olives in
    brine, drained

salt and pepper

freshly grated Parmesan cheese,
    to serve

1 Cut the asparagus into 5-cm/
2-inch lengths with a sharp knife. Thinly slice the mangetout diagonally and slice the French beans into 2.5-cm/1-inch pieces. Thinly slice the leek and reserve until required.

2 Bring a large pan of water to the boil over a medium heat. Add the asparagus, French beans and broad beans and cook for 4 minutes. Drain thoroughly, rinse in cold water and drain again. Reserve.

3 Bring a large pan of lightly salted water to the boil over a medium heat. Add the pasta and cook for 8–10 minutes, or until tender, but still firm to the bite. Drain thoroughly. Toss in 1 tablespoon of the oil and season to taste with salt and pepper.

4 Meanwhile, heat a large wok over a low heat. Add the remaining oil and butter or margarine and when hot, add the leek, garlic and tofu. Stir-fry gently for 1–2 minutes, or until the vegetables have just softened.

5 Stir in the mangetout and cook for 1 further minute.

6 Add the blanched vegetables and olives to the wok and heat through for 1 minute. Carefully stir in the pasta and adjust the seasoning, if necessary. Cook for 1 minute and pile into a warmed serving dish. Serve with freshly grated Parmesan cheese.

vegetable cannelloni

1 aubergine

125 ml/4 fl oz olive oil

225 g/8 oz spinach

2 garlic cloves, crushed

1 tsp ground cumin

85 g/3 oz mushrooms, chopped

12 cannelloni tubes

salt and pepper

TOMATO SAUCE

1 tbsp olive oil

1 onion, chopped

2 garlic cloves, crushed

800 g/1 lb 12 oz canned
   chopped tomatoes

1 tsp caster sugar

2 tbsp chopped fresh basil

55 g/2 oz sliced mozzarella cheese

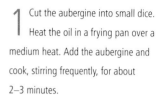

1 Cut the aubergine into small dice. Heat the oil in a frying pan over a medium heat. Add the aubergine and cook, stirring frequently, for about 2–3 minutes.

2 Add the spinach, garlic, cumin and mushrooms and reduce the heat. Season to taste with salt and pepper and cook, stirring, for about 2–3 minutes. Spoon the mixture into the cannelloni and put into a greased ovenproof dish in a single layer.

3 To make the sauce, heat the oil in a pan over a medium heat. Add the onion and garlic and cook for 1 minute. Add the tomatoes, sugar and basil and bring to the boil. Reduce the heat and simmer for about 5 minutes. Spoon the sauce over the cannelloni.

4 Arrange the sliced mozzarella cheese on top of the sauce and bake in a preheated oven at 190°C/375°F/Gas Mark 5, for about 30 minutes, or until the cheese is golden brown and bubbling. Serve.

macaroni cheese & tomato

serves four

225 g/8 oz dried elbow macaroni

175 g/6 oz freshly grated
   Cheddar cheese

100 g/3½ oz freshly grated
   Parmesan cheese

1 tbsp butter or margarine, plus
   extra for greasing

4 tbsp fresh white breadcrumbs

1 tbsp chopped fresh basil

salt and pepper

TOMATO SAUCE

1 tbsp olive oil

1 shallot, chopped finely

2 garlic cloves, crushed

500 g/1 lb 2 oz canned tomatoes

1 tbsp chopped fresh basil

1 To make the tomato sauce, heat the oil in a pan over a medium heat. Add the shallot and garlic and cook, stirring constantly, for 1 minute. Add the tomatoes and basil and season to taste with salt and pepper. Cook, stirring, for 10 minutes.

2 Meanwhile, bring a large pan of lightly salted water to the boil over a medium heat. Add the macaroni and cook for 8 minutes, or until tender, but still firm to the bite. Drain well.

3 Mix the grated Cheddar and Parmesan cheeses together in a small bowl. Grease a deep, ovenproof dish with a little butter. Spoon one-third of the tomato sauce into the base of the dish, then cover with one-third of the macaroni and top with one-third of the mixed cheeses. Season to taste with salt and pepper. Repeat these layers twice, ending with a layer of the grated cheeses.

4 Mix the breadcrumbs and basil together and sprinkle evenly over the top. Dot the topping with the butter and cook in a preheated oven at 190°C/ 375°F/Gas Mark 5, for about 25 minutes, or until the the topping is golden brown and bubbling. Serve.

courgette & aubergine lasagne

serves four

1 kg/2 lb 4 oz aubergines

8 tbsp olive oil

25 g/1 oz garlic and herb butter

450 g/1 lb courgettes, sliced

225 g/8 oz freshly grated
   mozzarella cheese

600 ml/1 pint passata

6 sheets precooked green lasagne

600 ml/1 pint Béchamel Sauce
   (see page 98)

55 g/2 oz freshly grated
   Parmesan cheese

1 tsp dried oregano

salt and pepper

1 Thinly slice the aubergines and put into a colander. Sprinkle with salt and leave for 20 minutes. Rinse and pat dry on kitchen paper.

2 Heat 4 tablespoons of the oil in a large frying pan over a low heat. Add half the aubergine slices and fry for about 6–7 minutes or until golden. Drain on kitchen paper. Repeat with the remaining oil and aubergine. Reserve.

3 Melt the garlic and herb butter in the pan. Add the courgettes and fry for 5–6 minutes or until golden brown all over. Drain on kitchen paper.

4 Put half the aubergine and courgette slices into a large ovenproof dish. Season with pepper and sprinkle over half the mozzarella cheese. Spoon over half the passata and top with 3 sheets of lasagne. Repeat the process, ending with a layer of lasagne.

5 Spoon over the Béchamel Sauce (see page 98) and sprinkle over the Parmesan cheese and oregano. Put the dish on a baking tray and bake in a preheated oven at 220°C/425°F/Gas Mark 7, for 30–35 minutes, or until golden brown. Serve immediately.

pasta with garlic & broccoli

serves four

500 g/1 lb.2 oz broccoli

300 g/10½ oz garlic and herb
   cream cheese

4 tbsp milk

350 g/12 oz fresh herb tagliatelle

25 g/1 oz freshly grated
   Parmesan cheese

salt

snipped fresh chives, to garnish

1 Cut the broccoli into even-sized florets. Bring a pan of lightly salted water to the boil over a medium heat. Add the broccoli and cook for 3 minutes, then drain thoroughly.

2 Put the soft cheese into a pan and heat over a low heat, stirring constantly, until melted. Add the milk and stir until well mixed.

3 Add the broccoli to the cheese mixture and stir to coat.

4 Meanwhile, bring a large pan of lightly salted water to the boil over a medium heat. Add the pasta and cook for 3–4 minutes, or until tender, but still firm to the bite.

5 Drain the pasta thoroughly and transfer to 4 warmed serving plates. Spoon the broccoli and cheese sauce on top. Sprinkle with grated Parmesan cheese, garnish with snipped fresh chives and serve immediately.

creamy pasta & broccoli

serves four

55 g/2 oz butter

1 large onion, chopped finely

450 g/1 lb broccoli, broken
   into florets

450 g/1 lb dried ribbon pasta

150 ml/5 fl oz hot vegetable stock

1 tbsp plain flour

150 ml/5 fl oz single cream

55 g/2 oz freshly grated
   mozzarella cheese

freshly grated nutmeg

salt and white pepper

fresh apple slices, to garnish

1 Melt half the butter in a large pan over a medium heat. Add the onion and fry for 4 minutes.

2 Add the broccoli and pasta to the pan and cook, stirring constantly, for 2 minutes. Add the stock, bring back to the boil and simmer for a further 12 minutes. Season well with salt and white pepper.

3 Meanwhile, melt the remaining butter in a pan over a medium heat. Sprinkle over the flour and cook, stirring constantly, for 2 minutes. Gradually stir in the cream and bring to simmering point, but do not boil. Add the grated cheese and season with salt and a little freshly grated nutmeg.

4 Drain the pasta and broccoli mixture and return to the pan. Pour over the cheese sauce. Cook, stirring occasionally, for 2 minutes. Transfer the pasta and broccoli mixture to a large, warmed, deep serving dish and garnish with a few slices of fresh apple. Serve immediately.

221

mediterranean spaghetti

serves four

1 tbsp olive oil

1 large red onion, chopped

2 garlic cloves, crushed

1 tbsp lemon juice

4 baby aubergines, quartered

600 ml/1 pint passata

2 tsp caster sugar

2 tbsp tomato purée

400 g/14 oz canned artichoke
    hearts, drained and halved

115 g/4 oz stoned black olives

350 g/12 oz dried spaghetti

25 g/1 oz butter

salt and pepper

fresh basil sprigs, to garnish

olive bread, to serve

1 Heat the oil in a large frying pan over a low heat. Add the onion, garlic, lemon juice and aubergines and cook for about 4–5 minutes, or until the onion and aubergines are lightly golden brown.

2 Pour in the passata, season to taste with salt and pepper and stir in the sugar and tomato purée. Bring to the boil over a medium heat, then reduce the heat and simmer, stirring occasionally, for 20 minutes.

3 Gently stir in the artichoke hearts and black olives, then cook for about 5 minutes.

4 Meanwhile, bring a large pan of lightly salted water to the boil over a medium heat. Add the pasta and cook for about 7–8 minutes, or until tender, but still firm to the bite.

5 Drain the pasta thoroughly and toss with the butter. Transfer the pasta to a large serving dish.

6 Pour the vegetable sauce over the pasta. Transfer to 4 warmed serving plates and garnish with a few basil sprigs. Serve with olive bread.

green tagliatelle with garlic

serves four

2 tbsp walnut oil

1 bunch spring onions, sliced

2 garlic cloves, sliced thinly

250 g/8 oz sliced mushrooms

450 g/1 lb fresh green and
white tagliatelle

225 g/8 oz frozen spinach, thawed
and drained

115 g/4 oz full-fat soft cheese
flavoured with garlic and herbs

4 tbsp single cream

55 g/2 oz chopped, unsalted
pistachio nuts

2 tbsp shredded fresh basil

salt and pepper

fresh basil sprigs, to garnish

1 Heat the walnut oil in a large frying pan over a low heat. Add the spring onions and garlic and fry for 1 minute until just softened.

2 Add the mushrooms, stir well, cover and cook over a low heat for about 5 minutes or until softened.

3 Meanwhile, bring a large pan of lightly salted water to the boil over a medium heat. Add the pasta and cook for about 3–5 minutes, or until tender, but still firm to the bite. Drain the pasta thoroughly and return to the pan.

4 Add the spinach to the pan with the mushrooms and heat through for 1–2 minutes. Add the cheese to the pan and allow to melt slightly. Stir in the cream and continue to cook, without allowing the mixture to come to the boil until warmed through.

5 Pour the sauce over the pasta, season to taste with salt and pepper and mix. Heat through gently, stirring constantly, for 2–3 minutes.

6 Transfer the pasta to a serving dish and sprinkle with the pistachio nuts and shredded basil. Garnish with fresh basil sprigs and serve immediately.

pasta & vegetable sauce

serves four

3 tbsp olive oil

1 onion, sliced

2 garlic cloves, chopped

3 red peppers, deseeded and cut
    into strips

3 courgettes, sliced

400 g/14 oz canned
    chopped tomatoes

3 tbsp sun-dried tomato paste

2 tbsp chopped fresh basil

225 g/8 oz fresh fusilli

125 g/4½ oz freshly grated
    Gruyère cheese

salt and pepper

fresh basil sprigs, to garnish

1 Heat the oil in a large pan or
ovenproof casserole dish over
a medium heat. Add the onion and
garlic and cook, stirring occasionally,
until softened. Add the peppers and
courgettes and fry, stirring occasionally,
for 5 minutes.

2 Add the tomatoes, sun-dried
tomato paste and basil and
season to taste with salt and pepper.
Cover and cook for a further 5 minutes.

3 Meanwhile, bring a large pan of
lightly salted water to the boil
over a medium heat. Add the pasta
and cook for 3 minutes, or until just
tender, but still firm to the bite. Drain
thoroughly and add to the vegetable
mixture. Toss gently to mix well.

4 Transfer to a shallow ovenproof
dish and sprinkle with the cheese.

5 Cook under a preheated hot grill
for 5 minutes until the cheese is
golden brown and bubbling. Transfer
to 4 warmed serving plates, garnish
with fresh basil sprigs and serve.

homemade noodles

NOODLES

125 g/4½ oz plain flour

2 tbsp cornflour

½ tsp salt

125 ml/4 fl oz boiling water

5 tbsp vegetable oil

STIR-FRY

1 courgette, cut into thin sticks

1 celery stick, cut into thin sticks

1 carrot, cut into thin sticks

125 g/4½ oz open cup
   mushrooms, sliced

125 g/4½ oz broccoli florets and
   stalks, peeled and sliced thinly

1 leek, sliced

125 g/4½ oz bean sprouts

1 tbsp soy sauce

2 tsp rice wine vinegar

½ tsp sugar

1 To prepare the noodles, sift the flour, cornflour and salt into a bowl. Make a well in the centre and pour in the boiling water and 1 teaspoon of oil. Mix quickly to make a soft dough. Cover and leave for about 5–6 minutes.

2 Make the noodles by breaking off small pieces of dough and rolling into balls. Roll each ball across a very lightly oiled work surface with the palm of your hand to form thin noodles. Don't worry if some of the noodles break into much shorter lengths. Reserve.

3 Heat a wok over a high heat. Add 3 tablespoons of the oil and when hot, add the noodles, in batches, and fry for 1 minute. Reduce the heat and cook for 2 minutes. Remove and drain on kitchen paper. Reserve.

4 Heat the remaining oil in the wok. Add the courgette, celery and carrot and stir-fry for 1 minute. Add the mushrooms, broccoli and leek and stir-fry for 1 further minute.

5 Add the bean sprouts, soy sauce, rice wine vinegar and sugar to the wok and mix until heated through.

6 Add the noodles and continue to cook until they are heated through, tossing with 2 forks to mix. Serve immediately.

pear & walnut pasta

serves four

225 g/8 oz dried spaghetti

2 small ripe pears, peeled and sliced

150 ml/5 fl oz vegetable stock

6 tbsp dry white wine

2 tbsp butter

1 tbsp olive oil

1 red onion, quartered and sliced

1 garlic clove, crushed

55 g/2 oz walnut halves

2 tbsp chopped fresh oregano

1 tbsp lemon juice

85 g/3 oz dolcelatte cheese

salt and pepper

fresh oregano sprigs, to garnish

1 Bring a large pan of lightly salted water to the boil over a medium heat. Add the pasta and cook for 8–10 minutes, or until tender, but still firm to the bite. Drain thoroughly and keep warm until required.

2 Meanwhile, put the pears into a pan and pour in the stock and wine. Poach the pears over a low heat for about 10 minutes, or until tender. Remove the pears with a slotted spoon and reserve the cooking liquid. Keep the pears warm.

3 Heat the butter and oil in a pan over a low heat until the butter melts. Add the onion and garlic and cook, stirring, for 2–3 minutes.

4 Stir in the walnut halves, chopped oregano and lemon juice. Stir in the reserved pears with 4 tablespoons of the poaching liquid.

5 Crumble the dolcelatte cheese into the pan and cook over a low heat, stirring occasionally, for about 1–2 minutes, or until the cheese is just starting to melt. Season to taste with salt and pepper.

6 Add the pasta and, using 2 forks, toss in the sauce. Transfer to a large serving dish, garnish with fresh oregano sprigs and serve.

traditional cannelloni

serves four

20 tubes dried cannelloni (about
200 g/7 oz) or 20 square sheets
of fresh pasta (350 g/12 oz)

250 g/9 oz ricotta cheese

150 g/5½ oz frozen spinach,
thawed and squeezed dry in
kitchen paper

½ small red pepper, deseeded
and diced

2 spring onions, chopped

1 tbsp butter for greasing

150 ml/5 fl oz hot vegetable stock

1 quantity Tomato Sauce
(see page 216)

25 g/1 oz freshly grated Parmesan
or pecorino cheese

salt and pepper

2 Mix the ricotta, spinach, pepper,
and spring onions together in a
bowl and season with salt and pepper.

3 Lightly grease a large ovenproof
dish with the butter. Spoon the
ricotta mixture into the cannelloni
tubes and put into the prepared dish in
a single layer. If you are using fresh
sheets of pasta, spread the ricotta
mixture along one side of each pasta
square and roll up to form a tube.

4 Mix the stock and Tomato Sauce
(see page 216) together and pour
over the cannelloni tubes.

5 Sprinkle the Parmesan or pecorino
cheese evenly over the cannelloni
and bake in a preheated oven at
190°C/375°F/Gas Mark 5, for about
20–25 minutes, or until the pasta is
cooked and the topping is golden and
bubbling. Serve immediately.

1 If necessary, precook the dried
cannelloni. Bring a large pan of
water to the boil over a medium heat.
Add the pasta and cook for about
3–4 minutes. It may be easier to cook
the cannelloni in batches.

tortelloni

makes thirty-six pieces

about 300 g/10½ oz thin sheets
    of fresh pasta

75 g/2¾ oz butter

50 g/1¾ oz shallots, chopped finely

3 garlic clove, crushed

50 g/1¾ oz mushrooms, wiped and
    chopped finely

½ celery stick, chopped finely

25 g/1 oz freshly grated pecorino
    cheese, plus extra to garnish

1 tbsp oil

salt and pepper

1 Using a serrated pasta cutter, cut 5-cm/2-inch squares from the sheets of fresh pasta. To make 36 tortelloni, you will need 72 squares. Once the pasta is cut, cover the squares with clingfilm to stop them drying out.

2 Heat 25 g/1 oz of the butter in a frying pan over a low heat. Add the shallots, 1 crushed garlic clove, mushrooms and celery and cook for 4–5 minutes.

3 Remove the pan from the heat, stir in the cheese and season to taste with salt and pepper.

4 Spoon ½ teaspoon of the mixture on to the centre of 36 pasta squares. Brush the edges with water and top with the remaining 36 squares. Press the edges together to seal. Leave to rest for 5 minutes.

5 Bring a large pan of water to the boil over a medium heat. Add the oil and cook the tortelloni, in batches, for 2–3 minutes. The tortelloni will rise to the surface when cooked and the pasta should be tender with a slight bite. Remove from the pan with a slotted spoon and drain thoroughly.

6 Meanwhile, melt the remaining butter in a pan over a low heat. Add the remaining garlic and plenty of pepper and cook for 1–2 minutes.

7 Transfer the tortelloni to 4 serving plates and pour over the garlic butter. Garnish with grated pecorino cheese and serve immediately.

spinach & nut pasta

225 g/8 oz dried pasta shapes

125 ml/4 fl oz olive oil

2 garlic cloves, crushed

1 onion, quartered and sliced

3 large flat mushrooms, sliced

225 g/8 oz spinach

2 tbsp pine kernels

5 tbsp dry white wine

salt and pepper

fresh Parmesan cheese shavings,
    to garnish

COOK'S TIP

Grate a little nutmeg over the
dish for extra flavour, as this
spice has a particular affinity
with spinach.

1 Bring a large pan of lightly salted
water to the boil over a medium
heat. Add the pasta and cook for
8–10 minutes, or until tender, but still
firm to the bite. Drain thoroughly.

2 Meanwhile, heat the oil in a large
pan over a low heat. Add the
garlic and onion and cook, stirring
occasionally, for 1 minute.

3 Add the sliced mushrooms to the
pan and cook over a medium
heat for 2 minutes.

4 Reduce the heat, add the spinach
and cook, stirring occasionally,
for about 4–5 minutes, or until the
spinach has just wilted.

5 Stir in the pine kernels and wine,
season to taste with salt and
pepper and cook for 1 minute.

6 Transfer the pasta to a warmed
serving bowl and toss the sauce
into it, mixing well. Garnish with
shavings of Parmesan cheese and
serve immediately.

aubergine & penne bake

serves four

225 g/8 oz dried penne or other
   short pasta shapes

2 aubergines

3 tbsp olive oil, plus extra
   for brushing

1 large onion, chopped

2 garlic cloves, crushed

400 g/14 oz canned
   chopped tomatoes

2 tsp dried oregano

55 g/2 oz mozzarella cheese,
   sliced thinly

25 g/1 oz freshly grated
   Parmesan cheese

2 tbsp dry breadcrumbs

salt and pepper

salad leaves, to serve

1 Bring a large pan of lightly salted water to the boil over a medium heat. Add the pasta and cook until tender, but still firm to the bite. Drain, thoroughly, return to the pan, cover and keep warm.

2 Using a sharp knife, cut the aubergines in half lengthways and score around the inside, being careful not to pierce the shells. Scoop out the flesh with a spoon, then chop and reserve. Brush the insides of the shells with a little oil.

3 Heat the oil in a large frying pan. Add the onion and fry until translucent. Add the garlic and fry for 1 minute. Add the chopped aubergine flesh and fry, stirring frequently, for 5 minutes. Add the tomatoes and oregano and season to taste with salt and pepper. Bring to the boil and simmer for about 10 minutes, or until thickened. Remove from the heat and stir in the pasta.

4 Brush a baking tray with oil and arrange the aubergine shells in a single layer. Divide half the tomato and pasta mixture between them. Sprinkle over the mozzarella cheese, then pile the remaining tomato and pasta mixture on top. Mix the Parmesan cheese and breadcrumbs together and sprinkle over the top, patting it lightly into the mixture.

5 Bake in a preheated oven at 200°C/400°C/Gas Mark 6, for 25 minutes, or until the topping is golden brown. Serve with salad leaves.

fried vegetable noodles

serves four

350 g/12 oz dried egg noodles

2 tbsp peanut oil

2 garlic cloves, crushed

½ tsp ground star anise

1 carrot, cut into matchsticks

1 green pepper, cut into matchsticks

1 onion, quartered and sliced

125 g/4½ oz broccoli florets

75 g/2¾ oz bamboo shoots

1 celery stick, sliced

1 tbsp light soy sauce

150 ml/5 fl oz vegetable stock

300 ml/10 fl oz oil for deep-frying

1 tsp cornflour

2 tsp water

1 Bring a large pan of water to the boil over a medium heat. Add the noodles and cook for 1–2 minutes. Drain well, then rinse the noodles under cold running water. Leave to drain in a colander until required.

2 Heat a large wok over a high heat. Add the peanut oil and heat until smoking. Reduce the heat, add the garlic and ground star anise and stir-fry for 30 seconds. Add the vegetables and stir-fry for 1–2 minutes.

3 Add the soy sauce and stock to the wok and cook over a low heat for 5 minutes.

4 Heat another wok over a high heat. Add the oil for deep-frying and heat to 180°C/350°F, or until a cube of bread browns in 30 seconds.

5 Twist the drained noodles with a fork and form them into rounds. Deep-fry in batches until crisp, turning once. Leave to drain on kitchen paper.

6 Blend the cornflour with the water to form a paste and stir into the vegetable mixture. Bring to the boil over a medium heat, stirring until the sauce is thickened.

7 Arrange the noodles on 4 serving plates, spoon the vegetables on top and serve immediately.

macaroni & corn pancakes

serves four

2 corn on the cobs

55 g/2 oz butter

115 g/4 oz red peppers, deseeded
    and diced finely

280 g/10 oz dried
    short-cut macaroni

150 ml/5 fl oz double cream

25 g/1 oz plain flour

4 egg yolks

4 tbsp olive oil

salt and pepper

TO SERVE

oyster mushrooms

fried leeks

1 Bring a pan of water to the boil
over a medium heat. Add the
corn and cook for about 8 minutes.
Drain thoroughly and refresh under
cold running water for 3 minutes.
Carefully cut away the kernels on to
kitchen paper and leave to dry.

2 Melt 25 g/1 oz of the butter in a
frying pan over a low heat. Add
the peppers and cook for 4 minutes.
Drain and pat dry on kitchen paper.

3 Bring a large pan of lightly salted
water to the boil over a medium
heat. Add the macaroni and cook for
12 minutes, or until tender, but still
firm to the bite. Drain the macaroni
thoroughly and leave to cool in cold
water until required.

4 Beat the cream, flour, a pinch of
salt and the egg yolks together in
a bowl until smooth. Add the corn and
peppers to the cream and egg mixture.
Drain the macaroni, then toss into the
corn and cream mixture. Season
well with pepper.

5 Heat the remaining butter with
the oil in a large frying pan over a
medium heat. Drop spoonfuls of the
mixture into the pan and press down
to form a flat pancake. Fry until golden
on both sides, and continue until all
the mixture is used. Serve with
mushrooms and leeks.

macaroni bake

serves four

450 g/1 lb dried short-cut macaroni

50 ml/2 fl oz vegetable oil

450 g/1 lb potatoes, sliced thinly

450 g/1 lb onions, sliced

225 g/8 oz freshly grated
   mozzarella cheese

150 ml/5 fl oz double cream

salt and pepper

crusty brown bread and butter,
   to serve

1 Bring a large pan of lightly salted water to the boil over a medium heat. Add the macaroni and cook for about 12 minutes, or until tender, but still firm to the bite. Drain the macaroni thoroughly and reserve.

2 Melt the oil in a large ovenproof casserole dish over a medium heat, then remove from the heat.

3 Make alternate layers of potatoes, onions, macaroni and grated cheese in the dish, seasoning well with salt and pepper between each layer and finishing with a layer of cheese on top. Finally, pour over the cream.

4 Bake in a preheated oven at 200°C/ 400°F/Gas Mark 6, for 25 minutes. Remove the dish from the

oven and carefully brown the top of the bake under a preheated hot grill.

5 Serve the bake straight from the dish with crusty brown bread and butter as a main course. Alternatively, serve as a vegetable accompaniment with your favourite main course.

vegetable pasta stir-fry

serves four

400 g/14 oz dried wholemeal pasta
  shells or other short pasta shapes
2 carrots, sliced thinly
115 g/4 oz baby sweetcorn
3 tbsp corn oil
2.5-cm/1-inch piece fresh root
  ginger, sliced thinly
1 large onion, sliced thinly
1 garlic clove, sliced thinly
3 celery sticks, sliced thinly
1 small red pepper, deseeded and
  cut into matchsticks
1 small green pepper, deseeded
  and cut into matchsticks
1 tsp cornflour
2 tbsp water
3 tbsp soy sauce
3 tbsp dry sherry
1 tsp clear honey
dash of hot pepper sauce, optional
salt

1 Bring a large pan of lightly salted
   water to the boil over a medium
heat. Add the pasta and cook until
tender, but still firm to the bite. Drain,
return to the pan and keep warm.

2 Bring a pan of lightly salted water
   to the boil over a medium heat.
Add the carrots and sweetcorn and
cook for 2 minutes. Drain, then refresh
in cold water and drain again.

3 Heat a large wok over a high
   heat. Add the corn oil and
when hot, add the ginger. Stir-fry for
1 minute. Remove the ginger with a
slotted spoon and discard.

4 Add the onion, garlic, celery and
   peppers to the pan and stir-fry for
2 minutes. Add the carrots and baby
sweetcorn and stir-fry for a further
2 minutes. Stir in the drained pasta.

5 Mix the cornflour and water
   together to make a smooth paste.
Stir in the soy sauce, sherry and honey.
Pour the cornflour mixture into the
pasta and cook, stirring occasionally,
for 2 minutes. Stir in a dash of pepper
sauce (if using). Transfer to a serving
dish and serve immediately.

three-cheese macaroni

serves four

600 ml/1 pint béchamel sauce
  (see page 98)
225 g/8 oz macaroni
1 egg, beaten
125 g/4½ oz grated Cheddar cheese
1 tbsp wholegrain mustard
2 tbsp chopped fresh chives
4 tomatoes, sliced
125 g/4½ oz grated red
  Leicester cheese
55 g/2 oz grated blue cheese
2 tbsp sunflower seeds
salt and pepper
snipped fresh chives, to garnish

1 Make the béchamel sauce (see page 98), transfer it into a bowl and cover with clingfilm to prevent a skin forming on the surface of the sauce. Reserve.

2 Bring a pan of lightly salted water to the boil over a medium heat. Add the macaroni and cook until just tender. Drain and put into a greased ovenproof dish.

3 Stir the beaten egg, Cheddar cheese, mustard and chives into the Béchamel Sauce and season to taste with salt and pepper.

4 Spoon the sauce over the macaroni, making sure it is well covered. Arrange the sliced tomatoes in a layer over the top.

5 Sprinkle the red Leicester and blue cheeses and the sunflower seeds evenly over the pasta bake. Put the dish on to a baking tray and bake in a preheated oven at 190°C/375°F/ Gas Mark 5, for 25–30 minutes, or until the topping is golden and bubbling.

6 Garnish the pasta bake with snipped chives and serve immediately on 4 warmed plates.

pasta mayo salad

serves four

1 large lettuce

250 g/9 oz dried penne

8 red eating apples

juice of 4 lemons

1 head celery, sliced

115 g/4 oz shelled, halved walnuts

250 ml/9 fl oz mayonnaise

salt

> **COOK'S TIP**
> Sprinkling the apples with lemon juice will prevent them from turning brown.

1 Wash, drain and pat the lettuce leaves dry on kitchen paper. Transfer them to the refrigerator for about 1 hour or until crisp.

2 Meanwhile, bring a large pan of lightly salted water to the boil over a medium heat. Add the pasta and cook until tender, but still firm to the bite. Drain the pasta and refresh under cold running water. Drain thoroughly and reserve.

3 Core and dice the apples, put them in a small bowl and sprinkle with the lemon juice. Mix the pasta, celery, apples and walnuts together and toss the mixture in the mayonnaise. Add more mayonnaise, if you wish.

4 Line a large salad bowl with the lettuce leaves and spoon the pasta salad into the lined bowl. Serve when required.

vermicelli flan

serves four

225 g/8 oz dried vermicelli
　or spaghetti
25 g/1 oz butter, plus extra
　for greasing
salt and pepper
tomato and basil salad, to serve
SAUCE
55 g/2 oz butter
1 onion, chopped
150 g/5½ oz button
　mushrooms, trimmed
1 green pepper, deseeded and
　sliced into thin rings
150 ml/5 fl oz milk
3 eggs, beaten lightly
2 tbsp double cream
1 tsp dried oregano
pinch of finely grated nutmeg
1 tbsp freshly grated
　Parmesan cheese

1 Bring a large pan of lightly salted water to the boil over a medium heat. Add the pasta and cook for 8–10 minutes, or until tender, but still firm to the bite. Drain, return to the pan, add the butter and shake the pan well.

2 Lightly grease a 20-cm/8-inch loose-bottomed flan tin with butter. Press the pasta on to the base and around the sides to form a case.

3 To make the sauce, heat the butter in a large frying pan over a low heat. Add the onion and fry until it is translucent. Remove with a slotted spoon and spread in the flan base.

4 Add the mushrooms and pepper rings to the pan and turn them in the fat until glazed. Fry for about 2 minutes on each side, then arrange in the flan base.

5 Beat the milk, eggs and cream together, stir in the oregano and season with nutmeg and pepper. Pour the mixture carefully over the vegetables and sprinkle with cheese.

6 Bake the flan in a preheated oven at 180°C/350°F/Gas Mark 4, for 40–45 minutes, or until the filling is set. Transfer to 4 serving plates and serve with a tomato and basil salad.

noodles with mushrooms

serves four

225 g/8 oz rice stick noodles

2 tbsp groundnut oil

1 garlic clove, finely chopped

2-cm/¾-inch piece fresh root ginger,
    chopped finely

4 shallots, sliced thinly

70 g/2½ oz shiitake
    mushrooms, sliced

100 g/3½ oz firm tofu, drained and
    cut into 1.5-cm/⅝-inch dice

2 tbsp light soy sauce

1 tbsp rice wine

1 tbsp Thai fish sauce

1 tbsp smooth peanut butter

1 tsp chilli sauce

2 tbsp toasted peanuts, chopped

shredded fresh basil leaves, to serve

COOK'S TIP

For an easy store-cupboard dish,
replace the shiitake mushrooms
with canned Chinese straw
mushrooms. Alternatively, use
dried shiitake mushrooms,
soaked and drained before use.

1 Soak the rice stick noodles in hot water for 15 minutes or according to the packet instructions. Drain well.

2 Heat the oil in a frying pan over a medium heat. Add the garlic, ginger and shallots and stir-fry for about 1–2 minutes, or until softened and lightly browned.

3 Add the mushrooms and stir-fry for a further 2–3 minutes. Stir in the tofu and toss to brown lightly.

4 Mix the soy sauce, rice wine, fish sauce, peanut butter and chilli sauce together, then stir into the pan.

5 Stir in the rice noodles and toss to coat evenly in the sauce. Transfer to a large serving dish and scatter with chopped peanuts and shredded basil leaves. Serve immediately.

244

hot & sour noodles

serves four

250 g/9 oz dried medium
      egg noodles

1 tbsp sesame oil

1 tbsp chilli oil

1 garlic clove, crushed

2 spring onions, chopped finely

55 g/2 oz button mushrooms, sliced

40 g/1½ oz dried Chinese black
      mushrooms, soaked, drained
      and sliced

2 tbsp lime juice

3 tbsp light soy sauce

1 tsp sugar

shredded Chinese leaves, to serve

TO GARNISH

2 tbsp chopped fresh coriander

2 tbsp toasted peanuts, chopped

1 Bring a large pan of water to the boil over a medium heat. Add the noodles and cook for 3–4 minutes, or according to the packet instructions. Drain well, return to the pan, toss with the sesame oil and reserve.

2 Heat the chilli oil in a large frying pan over a medium heat. Add the garlic, spring onions and button mushrooms and quickly stir-fry for 2 minutes or until just softened.

3 Add the black mushrooms, lime juice, soy sauce and sugar and continue stir-frying until boiling. Add the noodles and toss to mix.

4 Make a bed of shredded Chinese leaves on a large serving plate, spoon the noodle mixture on top and garnish with chopped coriander and chopped peanuts. Serve.

COOK'S TIP

Thai chilli oil is very hot, so if you want a milder flavour, use vegetable oil for the initial cooking instead, then add a final drizzle of chilli oil just for seasoning.

245

Desserts

If, when you think about pasta dishes, desserts
do not usually spring to the forefront of your
mind, you will be amazed by the wonderfully
self-indulgent sweet treats in this chapter, such as Honey & Nut Nests,
Raspberry Fusilli and Baked Sweet Ravioli. The Italians love their desserts, but
when there is a special gathering or celebration, then a special effort is made
and the delicacies appear. The Sicilians are said to have the sweetest tooth of
all, and many of the greatest and most delicious Italian desserts are thought to
have originated there.

honey & nut nests

serves four

225 g/8 oz angel hair pasta

115 g/4 oz butter

175 g/6 oz shelled pistachio
  nuts, chopped

115 g/4 oz sugar

115 g/4 oz clear honey

150 ml/5 fl oz water

2 tsp lemon juice

salt

Greek-style yogurt, to serve

COOK'S TIP

Angel hair pasta is also known as
capelli d'Angelo. Long and very
fine, it is usually sold in small
bunches that resemble nests.

1 Bring a large pan of lightly salted
water to the boil over a medium
heat. Add the pasta and cook for about
8–10 minutes, or until tender, but still
firm to the bite. Drain the pasta and
return to the pan. Add the butter and
toss to coat the pasta thoroughly.
Leave to cool completely.

2 Arrange 4 small flan or poaching
rings on a large baking tray.
Divide the pasta into 8 equal quantities
and spoon 4 of them into the rings.
Press down lightly with a spoon. Top
the pasta with half the nuts, then add
the remaining pasta.

3 Bake in a preheated oven at
180°C/350°F/Gas Mark 4, for
about 45 minutes, or until golden.

4 Meanwhile, put the sugar, honey
and water in a small pan and
bring to the boil over a low heat,
stirring constantly, until the sugar has
dissolved completely. Simmer for
10 minutes, add the lemon juice and
simmer for 5 minutes.

5 Carefully transfer the angel hair
nests to a serving dish with a
spatula or fish slice. Pour over the
honey syrup, sprinkle over the
remaining nuts and leave to cool
completely before serving. Hand the
Greek-style yogurt separately.

german noodle pudding

serves four

4 tbsp butter, plus extra for greasing

175 g/6 oz ribbon egg noodles

115 g/4 oz cream cheese

225 g/8 oz cottage cheese

85 g/3 oz caster sugar

2 eggs, beaten lightly

125 ml/4 fl oz soured cream

1 tsp vanilla essence

pinch of ground cinnamon

1 tsp grated lemon rind

25 g/1 oz flaked almonds

25 g/1 oz dry white breadcrumbs

sifted icing sugar, for dusting

1 Lightly grease an oval ovenproof dish with a little butter. Bring a large pan of water to the boil over a medium heat. Add the noodles and cook for 10 minutes, or until tender, but still firm to the bite. Drain and reserve.

2 Beat the cream cheese with the cottage cheese and caster sugar in a large bowl until the mixture is smooth. Add the beaten eggs, a little at a time, beating thoroughly after each addition.

3 Stir in the soured cream, vanilla essence, cinnamon and lemon rind and fold in the noodles. Transfer the mixture to the prepared dish and level the surface.

4 Melt the butter in a small frying pan over a low heat. Add the almonds and fry, stirring constantly, for about 1–1½ minutes, or until they are lightly coloured. Remove the frying pan from the heat and stir the breadcrumbs into the almonds.

5 Sprinkle the almond and breadcrumb mixture evenly over the pudding and bake in a preheated oven at 180°C/350°F/Gas Mark 4, for 35–40 minutes, or until just set. Dust the top with a little sifted icing sugar and serve immediately.

baked sweet ravioli

serves four

SWEET PASTA DOUGH

425 g/15 oz pasta or strong
   white flour

140 g/ 5 oz butter, plus extra
   for greasing

140 g/ 5 oz caster sugar

4 eggs

25 g/1 oz yeast

125 ml/4 fl oz warm milk

FILLING

175 g/6 oz chestnut purée

55 g/2 oz cocoa powder

55 g/2 oz caster sugar

55 g/2 oz chopped almonds

55 g/2 oz crushed amaretti biscuits

175 g/6 oz orange marmalade

1 To make the pasta dough, sift the flour into a large bowl, then mix in the butter, sugar and 3 eggs.

2 Mix the yeast and warm milk together in a small bowl and when thoroughly blended, mix into the sweet pasta dough.

3 Knead the dough for 20 minutes, cover with a clean cloth and leave in a warm place for 1 hour to rise.

4 Mix the chestnut purée, cocoa powder, sugar, almonds, amaretti biscuits and the orange marmalade together in a separate bowl.

5 Grease a baking sheet generously with butter.

6 Lightly flour the work surface. Roll out the pasta dough into a thin sheet and cut into 5-cm/2-inch rounds with a plain pastry cutter.

7 Put a spoonful of filling on to each round, then fold in half, pressing the edges to seal. Arrange on the prepared baking sheet, spacing the ravioli out well.

8 Beat the remaining egg and brush all over the ravioli to glaze. Bake in a preheated oven at 180°C/350°F/ Gas Mark 4, for 20 minutes. Serve.

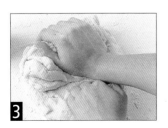

raspberry fusilli

serves four

175 g/6 oz dried fusilli

700g/1 lb 9 oz fresh raspberries

2 tbsp caster sugar

1 tbsp lemon juice

4 tbsp flaked almonds

3 tbsp raspberry liqueur

COOK'S TIP

You could use almost any sweet, really ripe berry for making this dessert. Strawberries and blackberries are especially suitable, combined with the correspondingly flavoured liqueur. Alternatively, try using a different berry mixed with the fusilli, but still pour over the raspberry sauce.

---

1 Bring a large pan of lightly salted water to the boil over a medium heat. Add the pasta and cook until tender, but still firm to the bite. Drain, return to the pan and leave to cool.

2 Using a spoon, firmly press 225 g/8 oz of the raspberries through a sieve set over a large mixing bowl to form a smooth purée.

3 Put the raspberry purée and sugar into a small pan and simmer over a low heat, stirring occasionally, for 5 minutes. Stir in the lemon juice and reserve until required.

4 Add the remaining raspberries to the pasta in the pan and mix together well. Transfer the raspberry and fusilli mixture to a serving dish.

5 Spread the almonds out on to a large baking tray and toast under a preheated hot grill until golden. Remove and leave to cool slightly.

6 Stir the raspberry liqueur into the reserved raspberry sauce and mix together well until very smooth. Pour the raspberry sauce over the pasta, generously sprinkle over the toasted almonds and serve.